SKETCHBOOK to STYLE

Discover Your Artistic Style in Your Sketchbook

might could

CHRISTINE NISHIYAMA

"It's thanks to you that I have filled an entire sketchbook for the first time in my life! I had never come even close before."

–CARLA F., SKETCHBOOK TO STYLE STUDENT

"I ended up completing six sketchbooks and starting three more. If I hadn't, I might have completed one or two sketchbooks. I have done perhaps more now than I have allowed myself at any previous time, except maybe early childhood."

–CRAIG A., SKETCHBOOK TO STYLE STUDENT

"Thank you for the amazing assignments so far. I'm finding my style and enjoying myself while pushing myself not to give up. I started keeping the sketchbook journal during the workshop and have not stopped drawing since. This has been an amazing journey."

–STEPHANIE N., SKETCHBOOK TO STYLE STUDENT

"Never had a sketchbook embarrassing enough and now that has changed. Since starting Sketchbook to Style with Christine, you can clearly see where I begin to totally loosen up and scribble. It is liberating. It wasn't until Christine have I found more confidence in myself. I don't ever want it to end."

–LINDA Z., SKETCHBOOK TO STYLE STUDENT

"Though I've taken collegiate-level art and drawing courses before, I had a really tough time being proud of my every-day drawings before finding Christine's classes. I can truly say she has been an integral part of finding my confidence as an artist so far. I have been drawing every day!! I know for a fact that what I've learned in just the first 5 sections of this course is what has given me the confidence to take on a daily challenge. Before I would have spent hours agonizing over the look of each of these guys, now they just seem to flow. I was never able to keep a sketchbook until following Christine either, that white-page fear is real!"

–KARA C., SKETCHBOOK TO STYLE STUDENT

"Not too long ago, people would ask me if I'm an artist and I would reply "not really", because… I felt like I didn't earn the right to call myself an artist. However, since joining I have finally accepted that "hey I am an artist!" I have more confidence in myself & my art than I ever have."

–MASINA S., SKETCHBOOK TO STYLE STUDENT

"And this is huge for me too: FINALLY, I have managed to keep a sketchbook, instead of thrown papers all over the place. As many described, it ended up to be one of the most deep and rewarding experiences."

–TATIANA M., SKETCHBOOK TO STYLE STUDENT

Copyright © 2023 Christine Nishiyama
All rights reserved. No portion of this book may be reproduced in any manner without written permission from the publisher except in the context of a book review.

Published by Might Could Studios
PO Box 92, Boone, NC 28607
www.might-could.com
First Edition
ISBN 978-0-9994039-1-4

The first version of the content in this book was released in 2017 as an online course. That course was taken by over 500 students, but there are some students in particular who I would like to thank for their hard work, inspiration, encouragement, and friendship:

Ann Snuggs
Becky Haystar
Brandon Baker
Carla Furey
Carol Choi
Christine Yun
Clint Johnson
Craig Austin
Dale Walker

Dawn Miller
Earl Harden Jr.
Jennifer Idleman
Jo Claire Mitchell
Julian C.
Kadazia Allen-Perry
Linda Lam
Lisa Hascall Kawasawa
Martin Morrison

Masina Sausi
Nick Harbaugh
Nikki Hemedy
Pauline McKinney
Richard Chin
Sarah Wechman
Stephanie Nunez
Suzette Craig
Tatiana Marza

Dedicated to every Sketchbook to Style class alumni.
Thanks for drawing with me, y'all.

Contents

Prologue: Why Sketchbooks?   i

1   Getting Started with Sketchbooking   1
Using This Book   1
Tools + Materials   4
The Sketchbook Manifesto   8

2   Freeing Our Hand   11
Training Hand-Eye Coordination   11

3   Making Marks Without Fear   17
Here's a Secret   17
Fear of the Blank Page   19
Imposter Syndrome   21
I Can't Draw What's in My Head!   23

4   Becoming Present   27
Relaxing + Slowing Down   27
Getting in the Flow State   30
Keeping Your Hand Moving   33

5   Letting Go to Play   37
Accepting Uncertainty   37
Enjoying the Process   41
Playing While Drawing   44
Accepting Mistakes   49
Iterating to Originality   53

6 Discovering Our Ideas   57
Looking at Our Memories   57
Paying Attention   64
Ideas Come From Actions   70

7 Exploring Our Voice   75
Drawing is About Seeing   75
Drawing from the Heart + Brain   80
Worrying What Others Will Think   88

8 Experimenting with Ways of Drawing   91
Representation vs Interpretation   91
Abstract to Emphasize   99
3 Basic Drawing Guidelines   101
Combining Words + Pictures   103
Tips for When to Use Words or Not   104
Word + Picture Combinations   104

9 Refining Our Visual Style   109
Your Mini-Me   109
Mini-Me Help + Inspiration   112
The 7 Visual Elements of Style   114
Style is Always Evolving   127

10 Doing the Work   131
Developing a Creative Habit   131
Your Drawing Space   136
Establishing a Routine   139
Perfection Does Not Exist   141

IT'S FOOD
FROM THE
GROUND!
HAPPY
INTERNATIONAL WOMEN'S DAY!
COME IN

Prologue

Why You Should Start a Sketchbook Practice

Hi! I'm Christine Nishiyama, illustrator and writer at Might Could Studios. I make books and comics, and I draw a whole lot. I've been drawing regularly for over 20 years, and drawing professionally full-time for over 10 years.

Over the past decade, I've taught more than 100,000 aspiring and established artists, helping them learn new skills, grow their confidence, and make more art. Many of my 25+ online classes focus on specific art techniques and processes, like composition and gesture drawing. I think these types of classes are valuable because learning and practicing new techniques and skills is an important part of improving and growing as artists.

But there's always been this other thing nagging at me, popping up in my brain over and over. And it kept popping up in the questions from my students as well. I've been thinking about it, writing about it, and drawing about it for years.

So what is this almighty problem that all of us creative folk have encountered?

You don't know what your artistic style is.

Or, put another way: you don't know who you are as an artist.

Prologue

If you're reading this book, you probably feel creative but believe your drawing skills just aren't up to par. You want to draw more. You want to be more confident in your drawings. You want to build a life around creativity and curiosity rather than self-doubt and fear. You want to stop telling yourself you can't draw. You want to stop sitting down to draw and instantly running into creative block, freezing up, and not knowing what to draw. You want to level up and be comfortable telling people you're an artist.

And you want to finally find your style and start drawing like *you*.

My Style Story

The solution to this problem is simple. Mind-blowingly simple. And I know because I've gone through this search for style, this search for voice. No one is born with a strong artistic style, knowing exactly the kind of art they should make. Your style is something you have to discover and something you develop by paying attention to it and nurturing it.

Each artist goes about that in a different way. And I want to show you the way I finally found my voice and learned to speak with it.

First, let's back up. Let me tell you real quick about my journey to find my artistic style.

- I drew a whole lot as a kid
- I took an AP Art Class in high school, got discouraged at how well everyone else could draw, and began to doubt my skills as an artist
- I went to college for Graphic Design
- I worked in a design studio for 1 year
- I freelanced as a designer for 1 year
- Then I took the jump, and transitioned to illustration full-time
- I struggled to find my style and voice
- I wallowed around in self-pity
- My bank account dropped to $100, and I got a part-time job at a grocery store
- I felt like a failure and almost quit, thinking I would never find my place as an artist or figure out how to make art that felt like me

But then, there was a huge shift in my creative life.

I began to draw like crazy. I was drawing more than I ever had before. I stopped trying to draw the way other people told me I should draw. I stopped trying to draw the way I read in books was the "best" way to draw. I stopped trying to draw the way other artists drew, stopped trying to draw the way I *thought* I should draw, and I started drawing the way *I* draw. I began to actually *like* the things I drew, and other people began to recognize my art as mine. I felt more confident in my art and in pursuing a career as an illustrator.

That was the year I discovered my voice and style.

That was the year I committed to a sketchbook practice.

And that was the year when everything changed.

Prologue

Two Ways a Sketchbook Helps You Find Your Style

So how did a simple sketchbook cause that creative shift and help me find my artistic self? There were two major changes that happened when I started keeping a sketchbook which led directly to that creative shift.

1. Love of Drawing

Ok, before you roll your eyes and call me crunchy, hear me out!

I believe that in order to become a master of a skill—any skill—you have to love doing that thing. Without that love, you'll never have the motivation, passion, or discipline to be able to commit to doing that thing consistently and put in the required effort to get good at it.

So, I believe a love of drawing is at the core of being able to draw well.

This may seem obvious, and you're probably thinking, "ok, but I already love drawing." But do you really? How often do you feel unhappy, stressed, or frustrated when you sit down to draw? Are you constantly worrying about making a "good" piece that people will like? A perfect piece that will finally go viral or sell?

Artists, including myself, often get stuck in a mindset of drawing based on external forces rather than internal forces. But I strongly believe that to find your own unique way of drawing, you have to learn how to draw for *yourself* and to love the process of drawing. You have to feel the drive to draw. You have to want to do it, to crave it, to feel it. You have to love it completely.

But the thing is, after we've been drawing for a while, focusing on trying to improve and get better, we start to lose that love for drawing. It begins to feel more like a chore, an assignment, a drag, rather than the invigorating, transcendent activity it used to be.

Love isn't something that just happens on its own. And once you love something, that love isn't always there in the same way. It can ebb and flow. Love is not a feeling—it's an action. A decision. A commitment.

Learning to love drawing, to *really* love it, is a huge part of finding your voice. It wasn't until I learned to love drawing, to truly embrace and accept the process of drawing, that I was able to open up and develop my unique style.

So how do we fall back in love with drawing?

> "The feeling of love comes and goes on a whim; you can't control it. But the action of love is something you can do, regardless of how you are feeling."
>
> – Russ Harris, writer + psychotherapist

2. Playing On the Page

We can fall back in love with drawing simply by playing. Yeah really, that's it! It's so simple, isn't it?

If we're thinking too much, taking things too seriously, or trying too hard, our quiet artistic voice can't be heard. It's smothered out by all our loud thoughts, expectations, and plans. It's trampled over by our ego.

Prologue

Play is essential to an artist's practice. Play is when we let go and fall into the flow. When we experiment with new ideas. When we explore other possibilities. It's when we allow ourselves to make ugly work. It's when we stumble onto new things we never would have otherwise.

And every time we play—even if we don't think we learned anything—we still had fun. We still enjoyed it and that joy cultivates a deeper love for drawing. That feeling of enjoyment, of love, is what will make us creative and open and able to hear our inner voice and discover our unique style.

> *"Play is a way of working and work is a way of playing."*
>
> – Sister Corita Kent, artist

Encouraging Love + Play

So if love and play are the only two things we need to find our style and voice, the question becomes: How do we encourage love and play in our art?

All you have to do is draw regularly in a sketchbook.

Over my years-long process of finding my own voice and style, I've discovered that keeping a sketchbook is the essential element that breaks down the drawing process to show you (or remind you) how fun drawing can be.

I know it sounds simple, but this new way of drawing has had the biggest impact and has been the most valuable change in my own artistic life. It took me years to figure all this out, and I want to save you from as much emotional stress, and years of wallowing in self-doubt and existential crisis as I can. That stuff's rough, y'all.

Our sketchbook allows us to focus on the joy of drawing, rather than drudging through principles and techniques to make us draw "better" according to other people's rules. Our sketchbook is where we play, experiment, explore, let go of expectations and worries, and it is essential to our growth as artists.

Your sketchbook is the key to focusing on the love, fun, and joy of drawing, and will lead you down the path to developing your style of drawing and learning how to draw like you.

Once you really commit to your sketchbook practice and follow through, you'll never experience drawing the same again.

Sketchbook Mistakes (And How to Avoid Them)

Before we dive into the full Sketchbook to Style strategy, I'm going to go over some common mistakes to avoid in your sketchbook. Just drawing in a sketchbook willy-nilly isn't going to help us find our style. We have to use it in a way that encourages love and play. And these mistakes below do just the opposite—they encourage feelings of inadequacy, guilt, and shame.

Mistake #1: I must draw every page in my sketchbook perfectly.

Let's get this straight: our sketchbook is not a place for picture-perfect, social-media-ready, crisp, clean, artwork. Our sketchbook is a place to make mistakes. To make ugly work. To just draw with no expectation of a final piece of art.

The act of drawing in your sketchbook is what's important, not what the final page looks like. We're here for the process, not the product.

Forget other people's sketchbooks. Forget the perfect pages. Forget everything. And just draw.

I'm giving you permission to make mistakes. In fact, I'm encouraging you to make mistakes. Go out there and strive for imperfection, let loose, and fill your sketchbook up with gloriously ugly, raw, true-to-you drawings.

Mistake #2: I need to have the most expensive drawing tools.

Maybe if I could just buy the pen that so-and-so has, finally my artwork will be as good as theirs!

Nope, that's not gonna happen. That person doesn't make good art because of the tool they use. They make good art because they make good art. And they could do it with whatever mark-making-thing you stuck in their hands.

So don't focus on the tools. They really don't matter when it comes to exploratory sketchbook drawing. Sure having a pen that moves across the page well and fits in your hand nicely is great. But it's not the end all be all.

A tool is just a tool. You're the one that makes the art.

Mistake #3: I have to draw for hours every day.

Before I started my sketchbook habit, I was always disheartened to hear other artists dole out the advice: "You should draw every day!" How could I possibly draw every day? I don't have time for that! I have to take care of my kid, work, make money, cook dinner, go to the grocery store, exercise, walk the dog... we all have an endless list of things we have to do.

I thought the advice to draw every day meant sitting down and creating a final, perfect, beautiful piece of art every day.

But that's not it.

It really is great advice to draw every day. And I'm recommending it to you right now, too. But here's the thing that took me forever to realize: you don't have to draw for *hours* every day. It could be mere minutes! Just drawing for 5 minutes is better than not drawing at all.

It's the act of putting the pen to paper that matters, not how long you sit down and do it each time. What really makes a difference is how *consistently* you do it.

Once you commit to a sketchbook practice, and you start drawing every day, you'll be surprised at how fast you grow and improve. Every time you draw, the next time comes easier. The lines flow out of your pen more naturally, you want to draw more, and you begin to crave drawing.

Do you see? It's a cycle! And it all starts with consistency. So try to draw every day, even if it's just a little doodle for 1 minute.

Mistake #4: I need to master perspective/shading/color theory/human anatomy/etc before I can focus on my style.

Many people begin their artistic journey by trying to draw things "correctly". Drawing perfectly accurate human anatomy or perfect 3-point perspective.

But this is just one way to draw, not the only way—or the best way, in my opinion.

Prologue

When you're drawing in your sketchbook, I think it's more helpful to not worry about drawing things "correctly" and instead draw from your heart. Draw how you feel. Draw your *interpretation* of that thing you see, not a direct representation of what you see.

It'll be very hard to find your unique voice if you're constantly just trying to mimic the world around you instead of slowing down and thinking about it for a bit.

So when you're drawing in your sketchbook, don't worry about what's good or bad, right or wrong. Don't worry about perspective, shading, or anatomy. Just slow down, listen, and draw what comes to you.

Mistake #5: I must make money from my art for it to be worthwhile.

First let me say this: I do believe art and money can be talked about together without degrading the art. If you are (or want to be) a professional artist, then you have to think about making money from it. And there's nothing wrong with that.

BUT. That is not what I'm talking about with sketchbooking. What I'm talking about in this book is finding your artistic style, finding your voice, and finding yourself as an artist. And to do that we *cannot* be thinking about money. Because money has nothing to do with finding ourselves—it will only get in the way and cloud our vision.

When we make money or popularity our goal, while we are still struggling to know who we are and what kind of art we make, we're setting ourselves up for inauthenticity and failure.

You can't let those external things be your primary goals when you're in the process of finding yourself and developing your artistic style. Money and recognition can only come after we've already discovered our voice and can already speak with it clearly.

Your only aim should be on the now. On doing the work. On this page of your sketchbook.

Relax, be patient, and do the work.

This is the only way to find out how to draw what can only be drawn by you. It will take time to get there. You won't find your voice overnight. But you have to forget about money. Forget about celebrity. Forget about other people's achievements. Forget about everything. Except you and drawing.

Keep drawing in your sketchbook, just for the sake of drawing, and one day, you'll see something original poking through. Your hands will begin to move without you telling them to, your lines will begin to form drawings you hadn't planned. Ideas will come that you hadn't thought of. Your work will take on new meaning. And you will begin to see your artwork as *yours*.

> "There's the drawing you are trying to make and the drawing that is actually being made and you can't see it until you forget what you were trying to do."
>
> – Lynda Barry, *cartoonist*

Prologue

Where We're Going

I truly believe your unique artistic style is inside you. Just like it did for me, a sketchbook practice can help you break through and find the artwork deep within you, empowering those drawings to flow out of your pen right into your sketchbook.

Hopefully you feel ready now to start your own sketchbook! I've taught plenty of art classes before, but this book goes deep into the creative process and really gets at the core of drawing. I'll guide you step by step through the process with all my tips and advice and over 60 drawing assignments. I'll show you how to start your sketchbook practice, keep it going, and use it to discover yourself, unlock your voice, and start drawing confidently.

The only question now is…

Are you ready to see how far a sketchbook can take you?

Sketchbook to Style

NOT SMILE
WEIRD
UMAMI!!
OH!
OH!
UMAMI!
AT A HAPPY HOUR:
WHAT BITCOIN IS?
it's fun to be
BAD
ALL DAY
+ ALL NIGHT
GRUMPY
1ST PIROZH
AI LUNCH + LEARN
NATIONAL HOT DOG DAY

CHAPTER 1

Getting Started with Sketchbooking

Using this Book

I'm going to jump right in and tell you the most important thing I will tell you in the entire book, and the most important thing you will ever hear in your life. Ok, that's a slight exaggeration, but it really is important and had a big impact on me once I accepted it. Are you ready?

There is no right way to draw.

We all get stuck in the mindset of drawing something "right", but there really is no "right" way to draw anything! Everyone draws in their own way, in their own style, with their own process. Artists use different tools, different routines, and different quirks. We're all different people and interpret the world differently, so we're going to draw differently too. And that's good!

However you draw is the right way. Just keep practicing and refining your own thing, and don't worry about how other people draw.

With that in mind, here are some rules to follow while completing this book.

Chapter 1: Getting Started with Sketchbooking

Rule #1: There are no rules in art.

Yeah, it's a paradox. Get used to it—art is full of 'em.

Rule #2: Draw every day!

I know it's hard to keep up with drawing every single day. We've all got a lot going on. But drawing consistently makes a huge difference in our artwork. Drawing is a lot like running, in that you can feel it when you haven't done it in a while and it's easier to get started the more often you do it. Just 5-10 minutes will do if that's all you have! Consistency is our goal.

Rule #3: Go through this book in order and do the assignments.

This book will be most effective if you read it in order and do the assignments as you read. I recommend completing one sub-chapter a day.

Rule #4: Don't over-exert yourself.

As I said before, we're aiming for consistent practice. If, while drawing an assignment, you find yourself tensing up, getting agitated and frustrated, no worries! Take a break, step away, or stop for the day. You already drew something today and that's the goal! You can always pick back up tomorrow where you left off.

Rule #5: No pencil!

Well, sometimes we will use a pencil in the assignments. But very rarely and not for sketching or planning out a drawing!

I know, I know. You really want to sketch out your idea first before you commit to ink. But drawing with a pencil is too hesitant. You'll end up thinking and rethinking every mark you make, trying to find the right one. That's not the drawing process we're looking for in our sketchbook. We're looking for a more instinctual way of drawing, the way of drawing that's natural and original to you. We're looking to make mistakes, *see* those mistakes, and learn from them—not erase them. If you mess something up, either accept it and continue on or start over again! Your way of drawing is inside you, we just have to stop overthinking long enough for it to be able to seep out and shine! So. No pencil.

A Note on the Assignments

I've written the drawing assignment instructions purposefully vague. They're clear enough to follow, but I don't want to tell you *exactly* what to do. This book is not about teaching you how to draw the way I draw, it's about teaching you to draw the way *you* draw.

So we have to leave things a little open-ended to allow that to happen. I don't give you completely specific rules to follow because I don't want to influence your artwork too much. I'm setting up some guidelines and constraints and giving you the freedom to explore. Interpret it as you will and let loose!

Please remember, there is no wrong way to complete these assignments. They can and should be understood in different ways. Yours will look different than others, and that's awesome!

Try not to worry about whether you're doing it right, following instructions, or doing what other people are doing. As long as you're *doing* the assignments, you're doing it right.

If you really get stuck on one assignment, don't let it stop you from continuing on in the book! Feel free to skip a few if they just don't click with you. You can always come back later and give it another go.

Chapter 1: Getting Started with Sketchbooking

Tools + Materials

Choosing your ideal sketchbook

Before we start actually drawing, let's talk shop. Your first assignment is going to go buy a sketchbook, and a few drawing tools, if you don't already have them.

But walking into an art store and staring at all the pen options can be overwhelming! In the future, I recommend trying out different brands, bindings, sizes, and paper types. Which one should we choose right now for this book? It's really up to you, and any sketchbook will work. But let's go through a few things you might want to consider when choosing a sketchbook.

The most important thing to remember when buying your supplies is that this book is about sketchbook art, not a final-gallery-ready art. Having good paper and good tools can make drawing more fun, but the tools don't make the art—you do.

We want to be able to keep a sense of play and experimenting in this class, so it's actually best not to buy super expensive stuff. I don't want you to be afraid to lay down a lot of ink because you paid $12 for that pen. We're here to draw, not save ink! So just remember, you can totally go cheap!

Binding

The first thing you should decide is what type of binding you want. There are three basic options:

- **Hardbound**
    - PROS: Sturdy, won't get smashed up, looks nice, some lay flat
    - CONS: Usually more expensive, heavy, some won't lay flat
- **Softbound**
    - PROS: Light, cheap, lays flat, can fold cover back
    - CONS: Paper is sometimes thin and bleeds, easily gets smashed
- **Wirebound**
    - PROS: Sturdy, won't get smashed, lays flat, can remove pages
    - CONS: Bulky, wire can get in the way

Size

The next thing you should decide on is size. This will be a personal preference, and you should choose what you think you'll like best. You want something big enough that you have room to move around on the page, but small enough that it will fit in your bag for when we go out drawing later on!

Personally, I usually have at least three different sketchbooks going on simultaneously: a large one at 8.5x11 in, a medium one at 5x8.5, and then a smaller one at 3.5x5. I use the larger one at my desk, the medium one in bed, on the couch, or in my backpack, and the smaller one stays in my purse or back pocket.

For this book though, I want you to just get one sketchbook and use that one book for all your drawing. A large or medium size sketchbook will be best.

Paper Type

The last thing we should talk about is paper type. There are all kinds of options, from smooth, thin paper to thick, watercolor paper. Your choice depends on what type of tools you're going to be using, and for this class, we're going to be using colored pencils, pens, and markers. So we need something that will work with those mediums. I suggest buying a sketchbook that says "mixed media".

If all this is overwhelming to you and you'd rather me just tell you what to buy, my personal favorite sketchbook is the Strathmore Mixed Media 300 Series sketchbook at 5.5 x 8.5 in.

But really, any sketchbook will work! Whatever you do, don't buy a super fancy $100 sketchbook. You'll just be afraid of using up the paper and will freeze! Grab a book and go—it'll be great!

Pens, Pencils, Markers, and Brush Pens!

Now let's talk about drawing tools! The tools you choose to use matter because they affect the way you draw. However, just because a tool is more expensive, doesn't necessarily mean it's better—especially for sketchbook drawing. This course involves a lot of experimenting with different ways of drawing so I'd like you to have the following tools before you begin. You may already have some or all of these, which is great! Don't feel like you have to go buy new fancy stuff for your sketchbook. (Remember what I said before!)

- 1 small set of colored pencils
- 1 pencil
- At least 2 drawing pens, often called fineliners
    - Fineliner pens have higher quality ink than a ballpoint pen and will draw a lot smoother! They have a hard nib and come in different pen widths.
    - I'd like for you to have at least two different widths:
        - 1 x-small or 0.1
        - 1 medium or 0.7
    - I use a few different brands:
        - Copic Multiliner, PITT Artist pens, and Microns
- 1 brush pen
    - This pen has a more flexible brush-style nib, and will give us really bold and expressive drawings
    - I use Tombow Dual Brush pens
- 1 set of basic markers
    - I use Copic markers primarily, but they're pretty expensive, and not necessary for sketchbooking or the type of drawing we'll be doing. Feel free to get a cheap set of markers with a small variety of colors.
- BONUS: This isn't necessary for the course, but if you'd like to experiment EVEN MORE having a white pen is fun for adding extra details on top of ink.
    - I use a Uni-ball Signo pen or Posca paint pen

Chapter 1: Getting Started with Sketchbooking

ASSIGNMENT 1.1
Get your sketchbook + tools

> Purchase or gather your sketchbook and drawing tools. Feel free to use any tools you already have—no need to buy new stuff if you've already got it! Not sure what brands to get? Go to *www.might-could.com/sketchbook-to-style-resources* for a more in-depth guide on drawing tools and my favorite art brands.

Sketchbook Manifesto

Throughout this book, we're going to be trying to get into a certain mindset that will allow us to explore, experiment, and discover. We're trying to get out of the self-doubting, technique-focused mindset, and into the flow mindset.

We may have to forget some things before we can learn other things. Here are a few of the things we should all remember while drawing in our sketchbooks. I'm calling this our Sketchbook Manifesto.

1. Slow down and be present
2. Give up control and stay open
3. Make mistakes and accept failure
4. Don't think and don't worry.
5. Be bad sometimes and be true always
6. Listen to and grow your Self
7. Make time for art and creativity
8. Play around and try new things
9. Watch everything and listen to everyone
10. Share your work and encourage others
11. Keep your hand moving and just draw.

ASSIGNMENT 1.2
Write your name and manifesto

1. Now that you've got your lovely new sketchbook and pens, write your name and date at the top of the first page.

2. Now let's write our manifesto on the first page in neat lettering. Take your time, but don't worry about it being perfect. If you'd like to add anything to the manifesto, go for it!

Why We Did It

Congratulations! You've just completed the first page in your sketchbook. Breaking open a fresh sketchbook and drawing on the first page can be daunting. We think the first page has to be really good, or else we've messed up the whole book, right? Nah, let's get over that. This assignment is a great way to make the first marks in your brand-new sketchbook. Who says we have to fear the blank page?!

FIGS
I STARTED READING
INFINITE JEST BY DAVID FOSTER WALLACE
IT'S VERY GOOD
AND UNIQUE, AND IMMERSIVE, AND I LIKE IT QUITE A LOT.
BUT MAN, IS IT LONG.
BREAK
I WONDER WHY PEOPLE DON'T WEAR HATS MUCH ANYMORE?
SOMETHING
IS
NOT
DAY 4 : NEW YORK
DAY 1 : NEW YORK
DAY 2 : NEW YORK
DAY 3: NEW YORK
AHA!
PERFECT
BORING
BLAND
BLAH!
POINT B
I ALREADY KNOW WHERE I'M GOING!
PROGRESS ≠ PROCESS
THE CREATIVE PROCESS
BOOK FACTORY

CHAPTER 2
Freeing Our Hand

Training Hand-Eye Coordination

A big part of drawing is improving our hand-eye coordination. Our goal is to not think too much while we draw in our sketchbooks. That's how we'll start drawing in our own original way. But to be able to do that, we have to be able to allow our hands and eyes to communicate clearly, giving us the ability to draw confident lines.

So let's do some exercises to brush up on our hand-eye coordination!

Chapter 2: Freeing Our Hand

ASSIGNMENT 2.1
Coloring for a New Mindset

1. Go to the back of this book, and choose one of the three coloring pages labeled Assignment 2.1. Tear that page out of this book and tape it into your sketchbook. If your coloring pages are missing, you can also find them at www.might-could.com/sketchbook-to-style-resources.

2. Color the page with your colored pencils while following the instructions below. Psst… a few students have "broken the rules" here and used different tools, like pastels, crayons, or even paint. If you wanna be rebellious too, I won't tell.

3. Color your page while listening to music. You can choose your own, or tune into our Sketchbook to Style playlist on the resources website from above. As you color, try to get as much dense colored pencil on the page as you can. Aim to use up your pencils as much as possible. There's no rush, lean in and take your time.

Why We Did It

This assignment helps us start moving our hands without actually "drawing" yet, so we can begin making marks in our sketchbook without so much inner criticism or worries. It also helps us get accustomed to doing something just to do it and get absorbed in the process. It helps us not focus on the "fastest" or "most efficient" way to do it. It helps prime us to be patient with these assignments, our art, the creative process, and ourselves. And lastly, coloring—a somewhat repetitive and mindless creative task—while listening to music helps us get into that mindset where we are not totally thinking and not totally not-thinking. We often think too much while drawing, and we need to learn how to get in the mindset of not overthinking. Because *that's* where creativity happens.

ASSIGNMENT 2.2
Practice Drawing Lines

1. Open your sketchbook and grab your pencil.

2. Draw one straight line, *softly* across the page.

3. Draw another straight line right below it, but press *harder*.

4. Try another pressing even *harder*.

5. Now grab your fineliner pen. Draw a straight line very *slowly*.

6. Then draw another line very *quickly*.

7. Now grab your brush pen and draw a curved line *slowly*.

8. Then draw another curved line *quickly*.

9. Draw a curly line slowly.

10. Then draw a curly line *quickly*.

11. Draw a zig-zag line *slowly*.

12. And lastly, draw a zig-zag line *quickly*.

Why We Did It

This assignment helps us in a few different ways. First, it helps us start moving our hands without actually "drawing" yet. We can begin making marks in our sketchbook without so much inner criticism or worry.

Second, drawing lines—a somewhat repetitive and mindless creative task—helps us momentarily tap into that mindset where we are not totally thinking and not totally not-thinking. We often think too much while drawing, and need to learn how to get in the mindset of not overthinking. Because *that's* where creativity happens.

Chapter 2: Freeing Our Hand

ASSIGNMENT 2.3
Tracing for Coordination

1. Go to the back of this book, and choose one of the two mandala designs labeled Assignment 2.3. Tear that page out of this book. If your mandala pages are missing, you can also find them at *www.might-could.com/sketchbook-to-style-resources*.

2. Place the mandala behind a blank page in your sketchbook. You may have to use a window with sunlight or a light table to see the image through your paper.

3. Now trace the design using your fineliner pen onto your sketchbook page. Go slowly, but don't worry about any mistakes you make and don't start over if you think you messed up. If you're drawing at a funny angle on a window, embrace that as part of the process! Just do your best with what you've got.

Why We Did It

Tracing to create final art often usually leads to stiff, lifeless drawings. But tracing can be helpful as an exercise to practice moving your hand and eye together, strengthening our hand-eye coordination. And doing this by tracing an existing artwork, instead of drawing something new, lets us do this without as much overthinking.

ASSIGNMENT 2.4
Drawing boxes for confidence

1. Using your pencil, draw 3 vertical lines and 3 horizontal lines in your sketchbook, dividing the page into a 4x4 grid. Don't worry about them being perfectly spaced out, and *do NOT measure it out or use a ruler*. We're not here to be perfect, remember? Embrace the wobble!

Your sketchbook page should look something like this:

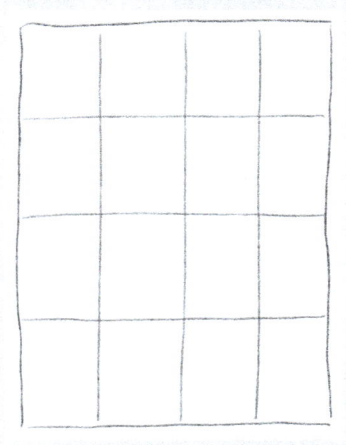

2. Now, in each section, draw a square with your fineliner pen. Try drawing some squares slowly. Draw some quickly. Draw some carefully closing each corner. Draw some not closing the lines, leaving the corners open. Try holding the pen tightly and drawing. Try holding the pen loosely and drawing. Just draw 16 squares in those 16 sections.

Why We Did It

All drawings start with lines and shapes. We're easing ourselves into drawing, starting with the basics, and working our way up. We need to let go of our preconceived notions of what our drawings should look like, and instead allow ourselves to just draw. We're just drawing squares y'all, there's no wrong or right way to do it.

WHERE WE'RE GOING
STATS
9 DAYS
2 PEOPLE
1 DOG
3,588 MILES
DAY 1
goodbye Atlanta
FIRST GRUMP
DAY1: New Orleans
DAY2: Houston and Beaumont
Texas
WATCH OUT! FOR RATTLESNAKES
the BIG TEXAN
STEAK RANCH
DAY4: ALBUQUERQUE
new mexico
the GRAND CANYON arizona
DAY5: ARIZONA
SALT LAKE CITY
DAY 7: BOISE, IDAHO
A DAY OF DRIVING
DAY 7: KENTUCKY
ECLIPSE!
DAY 7: ATLANTA!
WHERE WE'RE GOING
18 CITIES
3 NATIONAL PARKS
11 STATES
38 HOURS
2,635 MILES
DAY1: MONTANA
DAY 2: WYOMING
YELLOWSTONE NATIONAL PARK!
GRAND TETONS
DAY 3-4: SOUTH DAKO
BADLANDS
NEBRASKA + IOWA
DAY 6: MISSOURI
DAY 8: SEATTLE
THANKSGIVING!

CHAPTER 3
Making Marks Without Fear

Here's a Secret

I'm Afraid of This Right Now

By now you know that I don't believe in talent. Sure, people can have proclivities or tendencies to do certain things, but in the end, I believe a person's skill come from how much work and effort they put into practicing and improving.

If we buy the idea that there is no talent, then whether you're skilled at drawing or not is just a matter of hard work. And that's good news! It means it's all up to us! That means the ability to draw isn't just a gift that people are either born with or not. All we have to do is draw and we'll be able to draw!

Chapter 3: Making Marks Without Fear

But then, as we begin to understand this, the doubt and fear pour in. We think to ourselves:

- Everyone draws better than I do
- I'm not good enough at drawing to invest more time practicing
- I'm not a real artist
- I don't know what to draw
- I'm afraid no one will like my art
- There's no market for my work
- My art isn't important enough
- I don't have an art degree
- I'm too old
- I'm too young

Please understand that the only reason I can list so many of these doubts is that I have them all the time. Everyone does. I'm doubting this entire book right now! I'm scared that people won't like the book. I'm scared that other people are better at writing than me. I'm scared that people won't understand what I'm trying to say. I'm afraid my ideas aren't good enough for people to want to read them. And I'm afraid I'm both too young *and* too old!

My point is: Fear is a normal, ongoing, and healthy part of artmaking. You just have to accept that you'll always have at least a little doubt about your work, and that that's ok. You're going to keep having them, even the most recognized and established artists do. So the question isn't how do we stop having fear, but instead, what do we *do* with that fear?

Let's go through some common fears in art making and draw a little bit to break through these fears and doubts!

Fear of the Blank Page

First up is the fear of the blank page. This is the fear of starting a new project and (as fear tends to do) it often spirals out into larger anxious thoughts from there: Where do I start? What mark do I draw first? I don't know what to draw! I never have any good ideas!

Let's get this out of the way: You'll rarely have a good idea before you begin. If I waited until I had a "good idea" to start drawing, I never end up drawing anything!

Don't worry about what to draw. Just decide *to* draw, and then do it. The ideas will flow as soon as you begin.

For inspiration and ideas to come, they have to find you already drawing.

Chapter 3: *Making Marks Without Fear*

ASSIGNMENT 3.1
Drawing shapes and lines

1. Grab two light-colored markers, colors you can draw on top of easily, not dark colors.

2. In the top half of your sketchbook page, draw a bunch of different shapes. Any shapes! Just draw whatever shapes come into your head first. Some pointy, some organic, some larger, some smaller. Alternate between your two colors to draw the shapes. **Do this now before reading the next steps.**

3. Now look at your shapes. What do they look like to you? Take your fineliner pen and begin to draw lines on the shapes to make them into things. Draw squiggly shapes on a circle and it becomes a globe. Draw two ears, two eyes, and a long tail on an oval and it becomes a mouse. What things could your shapes be?

5. Now grab your markers again and draw the same shapes, in roughly the same arrangement again on the bottom half of the page.

6. With your brush pen, draw the outline of the things you created above. No small details here like whiskers.

7. With your smallest fineliner pen, draw the detail lines from the previous top half of the page that turn your shapes into things.

Why We Did It

If we're struggling to draw, it's often because we have a bunch of preconceived notions and beliefs about how we're *supposed* to draw. Those beliefs are limiting us and our explorations. We need to let go of those beliefs and allow ourselves to be open to different ways of drawing. We're just exploring. We're just drawing.

Imposter Syndrome

No One Knows

There's this thing called Imposter Syndrome, which is basically feeling like you have no idea what you're doing, and that one day everyone is going to find out that you don't know what you're doing, and reveal you as a big fake.

Well, I have some important news for you: *No one* knows what they're doing.

No one really knows how to be an adult (even adults), no one really knows how to be a parent (even parents), and no one knows how to make good art (even artists).

The trick, however frustrating it may sound, is to just do it.

Just pay your bills, and you're being an adult! Just feed your kid breakfast, and you're being a parent!! Just draw *something* and you've made good art.

You'll learn whatever you need to know along the way. But to do that, you have to begin.

ASSIGNMENT 3.2
Drawing squares of texture

1. Make a grid of 6x8 squares, leaving a small margin around paper. No need to measure, just estimate. It should look kinda like this:

2. Grab all your drawing tools. In the first square, draw a pattern or texture with whichever drawing tool you choose. Things like hatches, stipples, blotches, lines, whatever you like!

3. Fill all the squares with patterns and textures. As you move from square to square, switch which tools you use. Try drawing the same pattern or texture with different tools. Draw whatever bubbles up!

Why We Did It

During this assignment you may have gotten stuck and thought, "how am I going to come up with this many more patterns?!" But of course, there are endless pattern possibilities, and once you *decided* to keep drawing even when you *thought* you had no more ideas—you proved yourself wrong. You kept your hand moving, even against doubt, and somehow more drawings flowed out. We have to learn to push through our doubts to break new ground and explore all the possibilities.

I Can't Draw What's in My Head!

Maybe your biggest anxiety is something like: "M art never looks as good as I wanted it to."

Well that, my friend, is no excuse not to draw—in fact it's the biggest reason you *should* draw! Drawing is the only way you'll ever get better at drawing, and you'll never find the art you're meant to create if you don't keep making it.

Here's another important note from reality: You'll *never* feel like your skills are as good as you want them to be. But that's a good thing! You should always be striving to improve. If someone felt like they had truly mastered something, they'd probably stop doing it as much. We all keep making stuff because we want the next one to be better. And yes, I promise, even the masters feel like their skills aren't good enough sometimes.

David Bayles, a photographer and co-author of the amazing book, Art & Fear, told this story:

"After months of practice with his musical teacher, [the student] complained to his teacher, 'But I can hear the music so much better in my head than I can get out of my fingers.' And his teacher replied: 'What makes you think that ever changes?'"

The expectation for your work will always be better than what turns up on the page. And that's ok. It gives you something to strive for with the next piece, and reason to keep drawing.

Chapter 3: Making Marks Without Fear

ASSIGNMENT 3.3
Drawing opposites with color

1. Using your pencil, draw 6 pairs of circles, about 1 inch in diameter, with some space between each circle. It should look something like this:

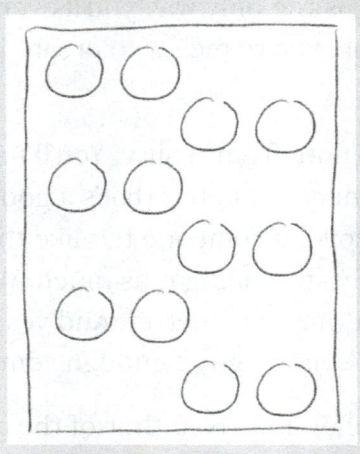

2. Now label each circle with the following concepts. Feel free to place the label however you like.

      Positive / Negative   Moon / Sun

      Darkness / Light   Autumn / Spring

      Aggressive / Timid   Winter / Summer

3. Using your colored pencils, color in each circle to represent that concept. **Don't *draw* things, just color.** You can use patterns and you can use as many colors in each circle as you like. For example, don't draw a snowflake for winter. You'll have to think more abstractly than that! Think about how color and pattern can be used to represent ideas.

Why We Did It

There are two perceptual qualities: concrete and abstract. Concrete perception is when we see, smell, touch, and taste with our senses. Abstract perception is when we think and understand ideas, qualities, and concepts. Concrete deals with things we can see, and abstract deals with things we can't see.

Ideas, creativity, and the art you haven't made yet live in the abstract world. This assignment helps us get more comfortable thinking and being in the abstract world.

MORE!
JOKER
HAPPY
INTERNATIONAL
WOMEN'S DAY!
WEIRD
shiba inu
Josie's
Burger
Saturday

CHAPTER 4

Becoming Present

Relaxing and Slowing Down

John Cleese, a British comedian and actor, developed a theory on creativity that he calls the Modes of Operation. The theory includes two modes: Closed and Open.

Closed Mode is an anxious, tense state, where we feel we have so much to do and will never get it all done. We are stressed, judgmental, and hard on ourselves. This is where our inner critic lives and thrives.

Open Mode is a more relaxed state where we're introspective and playful, allowing curiosity to bubble up, and pressure to lift. We are original, creative, and self-aware. This is where we draw like us.

We all spend a whole lot of time in Closed Mode, but original drawing does not happen in Closed Mode.

So how do we move from Closed Mode to Open Mode?

Practicing Mindfulness

Drawing, and being creative in general, is very similar to meditation or mindfulness. We have to quiet our thoughts so we can hear our inner voice.

Mindfulness is basically being able to pay attention to the present moment and recognize your thoughts without judging them. Being mindful makes us more self-aware, more focused, and able to see more clearly. It also allows us to be less judgmental of ourselves and others, regulate emotions, and reduce stress! All of these benefits are extremely conducive to getting in the flow state and being able to draw without worrying and over thinking.

Mindfulness is often practiced through Mindful Meditation which often involves being mindful of your breath, concentration, and being aware of your body.

Mindfulness and drawing also form a cycle. We can explore mindfulness by drawing and we can explore drawing through mindfulness.

ASSIGNMENT 4.1
Mindful Relaxation Line Drawing

Let's go through a short Mindful Meditation exercise using drawing to be mindful of our breath, concentrate our mind, and be aware of our body. For this assignment, you'll need a phone or computer to listen to a short audio recording.

1. Sit down at your desk, or wherever you choose to draw. Make sure you are alone and the space is quiet and free of distractions.

2. Open your sketchbook and set your fineliner pen next to it.

3. On your phone or computer go to:
www.might-could.com/sketchbook-to-style-resources

4. Listen to the meditation audio recording under Assignment 4.1, following the instructions while you draw along.

Why We Did It

This exercise helps us have a clearer mind and feel more relaxed. It helps us clear out the thoughts in our head, allowing us to be more focused and present, tapping into that Open Mode more easily.

Chapter 4: Becoming Present

Getting in the Flow State

The Flow State

Another name for the creative mindset we're trying to reside in is called the Flow State. Being in the flow is when you are completely absorbed in your work, so totally concentrated and devoted to what you are doing that you lose track of time. In the flow state, you are so involved with an activity that everything else drops out of focus. What you do and what you think converge. Your thoughts, worries, and inner critic fall away, and you just do.

Some people call this getting in the Zone. No matter what you call it, it's a complete absorption in what you're doing. It feels transcendent, meditative, and at one with the world. This is where you will find your voice and draw in the way that comes naturally to you.

In the flow, your self expands and dissolves away. You become both more aware of your self and more aware that your self is not quite as solid as you thought. You feel a sense of unity with the world. You feel tapped into something bigger than yourself.

When we're in our flow, we do our best, most original work. But how do we get there?

Internal vs External Rewards

As artists, we are often orient ourselves too much around external rewards like money, awards, or praise from others. If we can instead focus on internal rewards, we can enter the flow state much easier. When you're in the flow, external factors just don't matter because we are so focused on the present moment and the task at hand.

While in the flow state, we are both action-oriented and awareness-oriented. This gives us confidence and a sense of purpose. We are immersed in our task and this immersion releases us from our inner critic and worries.

Just as with mindfulness, getting in the zone can be achieved by being present and aware. We can notice what goes on inside and around us and be inspired. We can feel a sense of wonder and connection to the world.

To get into the flow, try doing these things:

- Try to let go of (or at least not hold so tightly to) your needs, wants, and goals.
- Trust in your ability to draw and be creative.
- Be mindful and aware of the world around you.
- And finally, don't give up!

Chapter 4: Becoming Present

ASSIGNMENT 4.2
Draw a relaxation spiral

1. Open up your sketchbook to a new page and grab your fineliner pen.

2. Put your pen to the paper, and hold it there—not moving—and take a deep breath. Slowly inhale and exhale.

3. Now begin to move your pen, drawing a tight spiral around the point you started on. Keep drawing the spiral out, ring by ring, keeping the lines as close together as possible without touching. Move the pen slowly, being conscious of your breath. If you run out of space, begin a new spiral on the same page.

4. While you draw the spirals, move your attention through your body. First, think of the top of your head, then bring your awareness down to your neck, through your shoulders, down your arms, through the tips of your fingers, back through your arms, down your core, through your thighs, down your calves, and through the tips of your toes.

5. Once you've completed your body scan, you can stop drawing spirals.

Why We Did It

The core idea for this assignment comes from the cartoonist, Lynda Barry. It helps us slow down, feel less stressed, feel more relaxed. It also gets our hands moving and gets us drawing on the blank page without having to think of something to draw.

This is a great exercise to come back to in the future if you feel like you have creative block, are having a hard time getting started drawing, or are just feeling stuck.

Keeping Your Hand Moving

What If It Just Stops?

Perhaps you've gotten in the zone, you're in the flow state, and you're feeling mindful and at peace. But then, your pen stops. Your line stops. The drawing stops. What now? What if we don't quite feel done yet? How do we keep drawing?

At this point, you need to keep your hand moving. To know what to draw next, or where to go next, you just need to start making marks. But what marks?

When you feel lost, it's good to have a simple mark making exercise to fall back on. These exercises give you something you can automatically draw, without having to stop and think. They keep your hand moving until we get a spark of inspiration that pushes us into the flow state again.

Chapter 4: Becoming Present

ASSIGNMENT 4.3
Draw the alphabet

1. On the same page as your spirals (if you have room), begin drawing the letter A. Write it big or small, in whatever style you like.

2. Keep drawing each letter through the alphabet, slowly and steadily. Try to calm your mind, be aware of your breathing, and really concentrate and focus on each line as you draw it.

3. You can complete the whole alphabet, or you can stop at any time and move on if you get an idea for something else to draw.

Why We Did It

Like the line drawing and spiral exercises we did before, this assignment is a great way to get our hands moving when we feel stuck. Often just getting over the fear of the blank page, and getting *something* down is the hardest part. These exercises help get us over that hump, and just get drawin'!

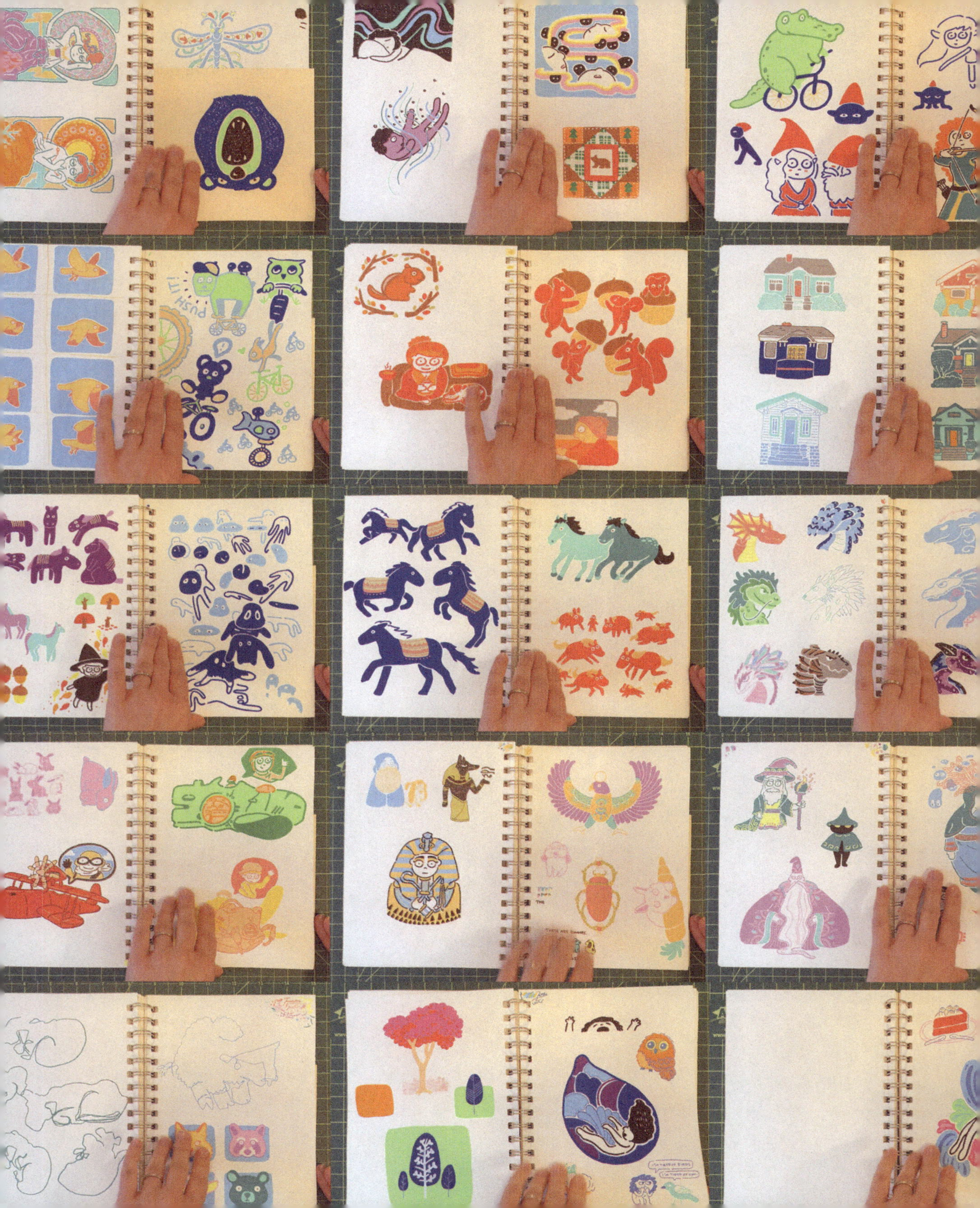
PUSH IT!

CHAPTER 5
Letting Go to Play

Accepting Uncertainty

I don't know about you, but I love certainty and stability. I love knowing exactly what is going to happen at what time, who is going to be there, how long are we going to do it, and most importantly: when and what we're going to eat.

In daily life, this habit of planning can be a strength. But in art making—when we're trying to draw freely, creatively, and uniquely—it can be a weakness. When I'm drawing, my craving for certainty and knowing what is going to happen is a flaw that I have to compensate for and actively try to push down.

This is because uncertainty is at the core of creating anything original and new. Doing something original means it hasn't been done before, and that means you don't know ahead of time what exactly it's going to be or how it will turn out. You can't plan it and you can't know.

If you only do things you know the ending to, if you only draw things where you know exactly what it will look like in the end, and don't allow for any changes along the way, you'll always end up with average artwork that isn't original, isn't true to you, and isn't pushing yourself. If you always stick with certainty and stick with you plans, you'll always go down the same paths and get the same predictable outcomes.

Chapter 5: Letting Go to Play

It's only when we embrace uncertainty, accept our mistakes as lessons to learn, and are willing to change our path and deviate from our plan that we can really be creative and draw in our own artistic style.

Beginning with No Plan in Mind

When I begin drawing in my sketchbook, I usually don't have a solid idea in my head. I just start drawing and the lines begin to take shape and turn into interesting things.

You've got to free your mind and just start making marks on the page. As you draw, happy little accidents will occur and then you seize upon those accidents.

Notice what works and what doesn't as you draw, what flows and what seems forced. Eventually, the pictures will evolve into something you never could have imagined in the beginning. They'll grow into something original and new.

In my opinion, it's this ability to experiment, make mistakes, and know which mistakes to keep, that makes someone a good artist. I believe anyone can draw, you just have to not overthink, put in the time to learn how the pencil moves in your hand, and be constantly observing and interpreting everything around you. These observations and interpretations are what seep into your work and make your drawings personal and unique to you.

ASSIGNMENT 5.1
Draw a Series of Squiggle Cats

1. Open your sketchbook to the next blank page.

2. Grab your fineliner pen and start drawing random squiggles on the page. Draw about 10 squiggles at varying sizes. Keep them simple and be quick—don't think too much about it!

3. Now look at the squiggles. Do you think we could turn these squiggles into cats? Try adding a pair of eyes to a squiggle. Now add four legs. Now add a tail. Hey, that kinda looks like a cat, huh?

4. Now make the rest of your squiggles into cats!

Why We Did It

This assignment helps us learn to embrace uncertainty while drawing. It also helps us draw in a way where we aren't thinking too much, and are looking at things more abstractly, focusing more on the process of creating, rather than the final product. It's also a great way to expand our ideas of what our drawings can look like, opening our mind to new possibilities.

Would you ever have drawn cats like those without this assignment? Probably not! But now you've drawn a completely original and unique page of cats unlike any the world has ever seen.

Chapter 5: Letting Go to Play

ASSIGNMENT 5.2
Draw a plane in time intervals.

For this assignment, we're going to draw a series of airplanes at a different time intervals. In the audio recording below, I'll set the timer and give you the instructions for each increment.

Aim to draw the whole plane within the time limit—don't spend the whole time drawing one wing! You'll need to draw faster at each interval to draw the entire plane within the limit. And *don't* stop the recording to look up images of planes—draw from memory. Don't worry about being accurate, or drawing a perfect plane. Just get some sort of plane down before the timer runs out!

Step 1: Turn your sketchbook to the next blank page, and get out your fineliner pen.

Step 2: On your phone or computer go to: *www.might-could.com/sketchbook-to-style-resources*

Step 3: Listen to the audio recording under Assignment 5.2, following the instructions while you draw along.

Why We Did It

This assignment forces us to draw more loosely and to abstract a subject to its essence. If you only have 15 seconds to draw a plane, what do you draw first? Which elements are necessary for a plane to be recognized as a plane? Which can be left out? This exercise also reminds us that we don't have to spend an hour to draw something interesting. Which of your planes are most interesting, the slower ones or the faster ones?

Enjoying the Process

To master a skill, you have to love doing that thing. Otherwise you'll never have the motivation or passion to be able to commit to doing that thing consistently enough and put in enough effort to get good at it.

So if you're ever drawing, and you find yourself unhappy, think about why that might be so. What are your motivations for drawing the way you are right now that make you unhappy? Are you drawing in the way you were told by someone else to draw? The way you think will make your work go viral? Based on other people's expectations and taste? Are you drawing what you think is the "correct" way to draw something?

You have to learn how to draw for yourself and to love the process of drawing itself.

The quickest way to block creativity is to be impatient. To expect to draw amazingly as soon as you pick up a pen. To expect to be able to rush the creative process. To expect to find something completely original and new, without having to struggle and work for it.

If you really want to improve your drawing skill, find your voice, and be able to draw in your own original style, then get to work. Start drawing right now. Focus on drawing something you love, that makes you excited and happy, and do more of that.

To become great at anything, you have to feel a drive for that thing. You have to want to do it, to crave it, to feel it. You have to love it. But love isn't something that just happens. Love is not really a feeling or emotion. It's an action. A decision. A commitment. An act of love. A commitment of love.

Learning to love drawing, to really *love* it is a huge step in finding your voice. Even if it feels like you lost the thread of love, you can have that feeling with drawing again, I know you can.

Let's just keep drawing and get there together.

Chapter 5: Letting Go to Play

ASSIGNMENT 5.3A
Draw cartoon characters

1. With your brush pen, draw lines to divide the page up into 4 boxes, something like this:

2. Write the name of a different cartoon character at the bottom each box, for a total of 4 characters. They can be any cartoon characters you like. Ones from your childhood or from now, old or new—it doesn't matter! Pick whichever ones pop into your head first.

3. Take a few minutes to do a quick internet search and find one image of each character. Try to do pick quickly, don't spend a lot of time here.

4. Now close out of your internet browser. No need to save the images or bookmark the page, just close it out and move on to the next part of the assignment!

Do this before you read the next instructions!

ASSIGNMENT 5.3B
Draw cartoon characters

1. Now, draw one character in each box from memory. Do **NOT** look at the images of your characters you looked up before. Don't worry about drawing perfect copies—*we don't want perfect copies*. We want whatever you remember in your mind. Try not to spend a whole lot of time thinking about it, just picture it as best you can and get it on the page.

2. Great work! Now look back over your drawings, and try to see any qualities that are repeated in your drawings, regardless of what the characters actually look like. Did you draw the eyes in a similar way? Did you draw a bunch of similar styles of feet? How did you draw their hair? Body proportions?

Why We Did It

Drawing from memory without reference like this forces us to draw without perfection. If I had told you to draw the characters while looking at the reference images, you most likely would have struggled and worried about getting things "just right". You would have been aiming to make an exact copy of the image, rather than drawing in your own way.

When we draw from memory (and later our imagination) we're able to let some of ourselves flow out into the art, rather than just copying someone else's art. We're able to let our instincts flow, and see snippets of our style come through. Copying is a great way to practice technique and strengthen our hand-eye coordination, but it won't help us find our unique style. Drawing without reference takes practice, but that's why we're here!

Don't worry if you're not happy with how your characters turned out. We're still practicing, and this is all part of learning and growing. You're doing great. Keep up the hard work!

Chapter 5: Letting Go to Play

Playing While Drawing

Sketchbook to Play

Play is another integral part of finding our voice and artistic style. If we're thinking too much, being too serious, or trying to hard, our voice won't come out. It will be smothered by all our thoughts, expectations, and plans.

That's why a sketchbook is so essential to an artist's practice. Our sketchbook is where we play. It's where we experiment with new ideas. It's where we explore our thoughts. It's where we make ugly work. It's where we stumble onto new things. And no matter what, even if we didn't learn something while playing, we still had fun. We still enjoyed it, and cultivated a deeper love for drawing. And that enjoyment, that love, is what will make us creative and open and able to hear our voice and discover our style.

Chapter 5: Letting Go to Play

ASSIGNMENT 5.4
Draw a pirate ship in time intervals

We're going to do another time interval drawing exercise, but this time I want *you* to do the timing! You don't need me to do drawing intervals—you can do them on your own too.

1. Grab a timer and fineliner pen. I use the timer app on my phone. Google has a simple timer function too, if you're on a computer.

2. Divide the page up into 9 sections, a 3x3 grid like this:

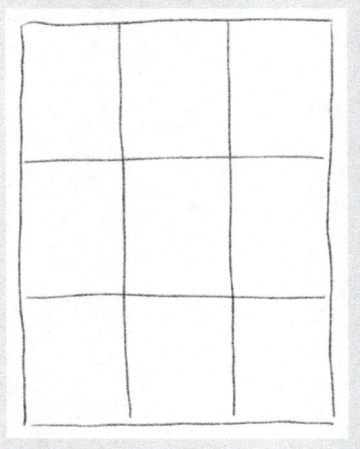

In each box, we're going to draw a pirate ship at different time intervals, just like in the plane drawing assignment.

Yeah, I know—a pirate ship! So complex, so scary... what does a pirate ship even look like?! Don't worry. And **DO NOT look up reference images before you start**. We want this baby straight from your memory and imagination. It *will* look weird. It *will* look wonky. That's exactly what we want.

So grab your timer and let's get drawing!

3. Set your timer to 3 minutes, hit go, and draw a pirate ship using the entire 3 minutes. Remember to draw the whole pirate ship within the time limit! Ready, go!

4. Now set your timer to 2 minutes, hit go, and draw a pirate ship within the time limit.

5. Now set your timer to 1 minute and draw.

6. Now set your timer to 45 seconds and draw.

7. Now set your timer to 30 seconds and draw.

8. Now set your timer to 20 seconds and draw.

9. Now set your timer to 15 seconds and draw.

10. Now set your timer to 10 seconds and draw.

11. Now set your timer to 5 seconds and draw.

Awesome work! Look at all those pirate ships!

Why We Did It

Like the plane exercise before, drawing at timed intervals is a great way to draw more loosely and practice abstracting a subject to its essence. It also proves to us that we can draw more things than we might have thought we could (hey, you CAN draw a pirate ship in 10 seconds!). Lastly, it helps us stop aiming for perfection, and instead encourages us to notice, accept, and love the imperfections that make our drawings OUR drawings.

Chapter 5: Letting Go to Play

ASSIGNMENT 5.5
Draw a page of simple facial expressions.

1. With your fineliner pen, in the top left-hand corner of the page, draw a small head with two eyes and a nose however you like.

2. Now move to the right and draw the same head again with the same nose and same eyes.

3. Keep moving over, drawing the head over and over in a row across the page. Take your time, no need to rush, but don't think too much.

4. When you reach the edge of the page start a new row and start varying the eyes from head to head. Change them however you like: size, shape, intensity, placement, spacing.

5. Continue drawing heads this way until you've filled up the page. Let one eye suggest the next. Experiment!

Why We Did It

This assignment encourages us to ideate while drawing, exploring different ways of drawing facial expressions, riffing on our ideas as we go, letting one idea lead to the next. We're aiming to become more comfortable with experimentation and practice coming up with lots of new and different ideas.

Creativity is about making new connections between different things. Ideating through drawing (ie. drawing lots of different versions of something) is a great way to create new and original connections.

This exercise also helps us focus on the process, not the final product. The point of this exercise is not the last face you draw, or the face you like best. The point is the experimentation, the exploration. The process is the point.

Accepting Failure + Mistakes

Mistakes Are Part of Artmaking

Striving for perfection in your artwork is a waste of time. It's simple: perfection does not exist. Someone (including you) will always be able to find something wrong with everything you make, no matter how long you spend working on it.

So we might as well just give in to imperfection and try to be more comfortable making mistakes.

I could go through every piece of work in my portfolio and show you tons of things I would change if I were to go back and draw them again. But at some point, you just have to let it go, call it done, and move on to the next piece.

Each piece of art you make won't be perfect, but you'll be a better artist than you were before you made each one.

Mistakes Lead to Solutions

There's a story about perfection I love from the book *Art & Fear*, by David Bayles and Ted Orland.

The story goes like this: a ceramics teacher split his class into two groups to test a theory. He told the first group they would be graded based only on the *quantity* of work made, while the second group would be graded on their work's *quality*. The first group would have everything they made simply weighed to determine their grade, while the second group had to create a single perfect piece to get an A.

When it came time to grade, a surprising thing happened. The highest quality work came from the group being graded for quantity.

While the quantity group was busy *making* piece after piece (learning from their mistakes each time and trying new things), the quality group just sat there *thinking* about what makes the best piece and in the end didn't have much to show for their thoughts.

This is a great example of how imperfection and mistakes are not just common in art making, but are actually an essential part of the artmaking process. You have to make a whole lot of bad drawings before you can make the really good drawings.

So don't be afraid to make mistakes, they just show you're doing the work.

ASSIGNMENT 5.6
Draw a book

1. Think of a non-illustrated book you've read that you loved. A novel or chapter book from a long time ago or from recently.

2. On the next blank page in your sketchbook, using your fineliner or brush pen, write the name of that book at the top of the page.

3. Draw an illustration that conveys the **entire** book. But I don't want you to draw every scene from the book. I want you to draw the essence of the book. The themes, tone, mood, personality, the story.

Think about how to simplify and reduce the book to its core and communicate that visually. Think about how to tell the story in one image. The final drawing could be very abstract or it can very detailed. You can include dialogue and a caption or it can be wordless. It can be small or large. Color or black and white. Have fun with it!

Why We Did It

This assignment helps us explore how to reduce a concept down to its essence, and to communicate that essence visually. We're digging deeper into drawing, y'all!

Chapter 5: Letting Go to Play

ASSIGNMENT 5.7
Cathartic doodling

That was a difficult assignment, I know! Let's let out some steam and tension by doing some cathartic doodles.

Sometimes when I feel really tense or stressed, I'll draw an entire page of nonsense. Just doodling whatever comes to mind, each line leading to the next, not caring what I draw, how bad it is, or how weird it is. Sometimes (if I'm being a big grump) it's just one angsty scribble! I always feel better afterwards—it's like a natural pressure valve. Let's do it now!

1. Draw a cathartic doodle page on the next blank page in your book. And you know what, let's go wild. Feel free to use any tools you'd like on this page: colored pencils, markers, whatever! Let it all out! Try to fit elements together, filling up the whole page.

If you get stuck and don't know what to draw next, remember you can draw spirals or the alphabet to keep your hand moving until something pops up! **Your only goal is to fill the page with a dense amount of drawings.**

Let loose and have fun!

Why We Did It

This assignment encourages us to draw just to draw. The focus here is on the process of drawing, and we're using that process to destress and clear our mind.

Iterating Our Way to Originality

Iterating Variety

So by now, we've accepted that mistakes and lots of drawings are what lead us to good drawings, but how do we get to those good drawings?

By iterating! Each time you draw something you don't like, take a quick look at it before you dismiss it. Why did you label it a "bad" drawing? Is it really so bad? There must be something good about it. What about that one line there? Or the way you drew that eye? Or what about that thick line over there? That's kinda cool, right?

If we take something and draw it over and over, looking at each one, choosing to keep the things we like, throwing out the things we don't like, and continuing to draw it over and over, iterating each time, drawing each just a little bit different... that's how we make gold.

And that's why we're drawing in pen. If you erase all your mistakes, you'll never see them and learn from them. And you'll never spot the mistakes that actually kinda work and that you actually kinda like!

Chapter 5: Letting Go to Play

ASSIGNMENT 5.8
Draw a page of head iterations

1. Using a pen, divide your next page up into 15 sections, 3x5.

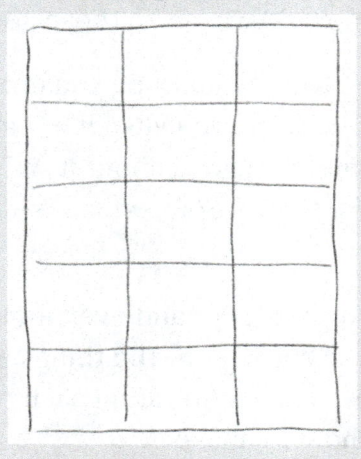

2. In the first section, draw a simple head and face. Don't overthink it, just draw a circle, two eyes, a nose, and a mouth. We just want somewhere to begin.

3. In each of the remaining sections, keep drawing that head, iterating and changing it a little bit each time. Let one head lead to the next, giving you ideas on what to keep or what to change. Did you accidentally make a stray mark on the chin? Draw the next head with a beard! Try to vary the heads as much as you can, ending up with a huge range of heads that span all kinds of differences. Girl, boy, human, animal, big, small, smooth, bumpy, cute, scary, anything goes!

Why We Did It

Remember, iterating is how we find our truly original ideas. We're learning to see our mistakes with each version, deciding which ones to keep and which ones to toss. I bet as you drew more heads they got more original and weird as you went along, huh?

ASSIGNMENT 5.9
Draw a page of bug iterations

1. With whichever tool you'd like, draw as many bugs on one page as you can. Yeah, bugs! Don't look up references, just draw from memory. Don't worry about drawing specific species or types of bugs—we're not aiming for accuracy here, just variety. Start with the first boring idea you have, and then iterate from there, changing each bug as you go.

Think about different styles of drawing. Draw the silhouette, draw in lines only, draw in shapes only—whatever! Just fill the page with iterations of bugs.

Why We Did It

Like the last assignment, this exercise helps us begin iterating and exploring new ideas and ways of drawing the same subject. Did you get a page of really funky bugs?

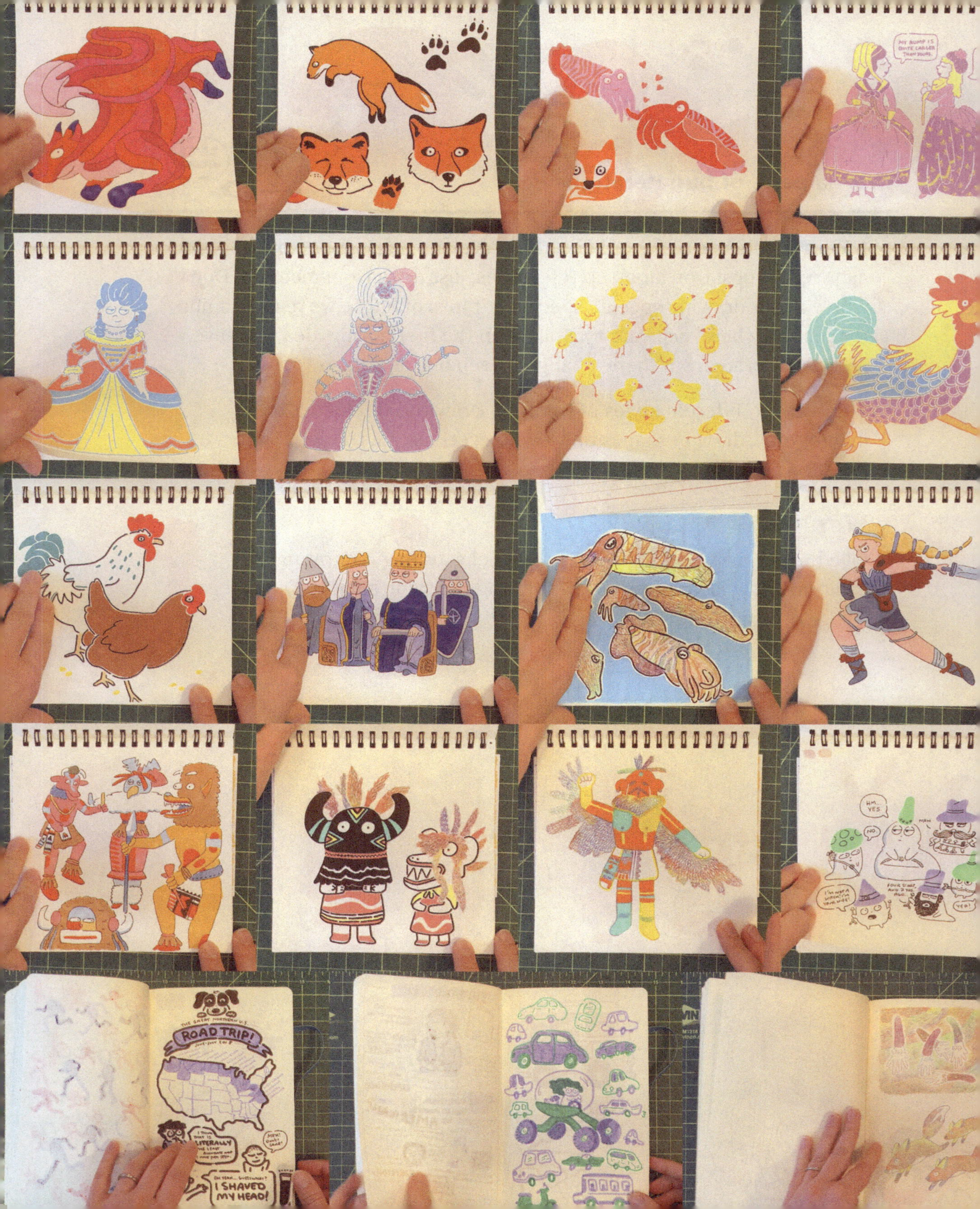
HM... YES.
NO.
NAH
YEP!
ROAD TRIP!
I SHAVED MY HEAD!

CHAPTER 6

Discovering Our Ideas

Looking at Our Memories

What Does Your Sponge Hold?

Our Self is like a sponge. We soak up everything we see and everything we experience. The choices we make, thoughts we think, feelings we feel, stories we write, drawings we draw—all of this comes from the sponge of our Self.

The more we experience, the more our sponge soaks up and the more we have to work with as artists. The more we get out into the world and expand our mind with new ideas, points of views and experiences, the more our sponge expands. Traveling the world would do this drastically, but you can expand your sponge no matter where you are by just being aware of the immense world in your own backyard.

Our sponge is filled with everything we know, everything we learn, everything we've thought, and everything we've experienced. Every book we've read. Every film we've watched. Every laugh and every kiss. Every sigh and every tear. And not just yours, but everyone else's that you've seen or shared as well.

These are all the things that make us who we are. We have all had completely different experiences and we are all completely unique and different people. We each have our own voice and to find it, we have to listen. We have to squeeze that sponge and really look at what comes out. What have we stored in there? What have we held on to all these years?

When you begin thinking introspectively, become more self-aware, and explore your Self, you'll be amazed at what you might discover. Our sponge is a treasure chest of originality and creativity just waiting to be explored.

Looking Back and Examining Ourselves

We've been talking about and practicing paying attention to the world around us, examining the world and noticing what we notice.

But we also need to examine ourselves, what goes on inside us, where we came from, and what we remember from long ago.

Your childhood experiences had a big impact on who you are today. You were very impressionable at a young age, so the things you saw, heard, and did in those years stick with you. I can be helpful to reflect back on our childhood memories and interests to discover new things about ourselves.

Ideas and inspiration don't come out of thin air, they come from inside us—from things we notice or remember. So let's look back at some things we remember.

To Find Your Voice, You Have to Be Honest

Most childhoods are filled with big emotions. Perhaps there was a traumatic event early in your life, a messy divorce, school yard bullying, or just the day-to-day tough situations of growing up.

Childhood can still feel raw in our memory years later.

But the only way for us to discover our inner voice is to be honest about our memories and feelings. The hardest memories and emotions are often the ones that hold the deepest truths, so try not to ignore them.

We need to face our feelings, both good and bad, and accept them for what they are. The only way you can develop your voice is by being honest about what's inside you. So how do we accept our feelings?

We have to acknowledge them and sit with them.

While remembering something, if we feel a past emotion again—whether happy or sad, excited or mad—acknowledge how you felt in that moment and how you feel about it now. Remind yourself that all these experiences and emotions made you who you are today. Here with our memories it's just us and we can work on accepting ourselves in this space.

If we can honestly reflect back on our memories, thoughts, hopes, dreams, loves, hates, and passions, we'll be on the right path to finding our inner voice.

Chapter 6: Discovering Our Ideas

ASSIGNMENT 6.1
The Things I Loved

1. Open your sketchbook to the next page and divide it into 4 sections.

2. Write a small label at the bottom of each section, with the following categories: Book, Movie, Character, and Subject.

3. Take a moment to think about your favorite childhood book, movie, character, and subject. Your favorite character could be a cartoon character, story character, or TV character, for example. Your favorite subject could be Dinosaurs, Trucks, Greek Mythology, or any other obsession you may have had as a child.

4. Draw each of those favorite things inside the box. Don't worry about creating a masterpiece or capturing the whole thing in one image. You could draw the cover of your favorite book, a scene from your favorite movie, or your favorite dinosaur!

Why We Did This

We're most impressionable when we're kids, and looking back on our favorite things from our childhood can give us an interesting glimpse into who we are today as well. These books, movies, and characters are often some of our strongest visual influences. If we can recognize and remember what those key influences are, we can use that knowledge to learn about and develop our artistic style and the art we make.

ASSIGNMENT 6.2
Who Am I?

1. Read the questions below and choose the one that calls to you most.

- What's the first movie you remember watching?
- What's the first book you remember reading?
- What's the first thing you remember that left you amazed?
- What's the first obsession you can remember having?
- What did you want to be when you grew up?
- What was the best present you received as a child?
- Who did you look up to most when you were young?

2. Think about your answer to the question you chose.

3. Using your fineliner or brush pen, draw your answer. This is pretty open-ended on purpose! You can go simple or detailed, abstract or straight-forward.

Why We Did It

I believe who you are is a huge part of what your style looks like. So one aspect of what we're aiming to do in this course is to uncover the story of you. Your story is your art. Your art is your story. You are your art, and your art is you. So what makes you, you?

Chapter 6: Discovering Our Ideas

ASSIGNMENT 6.3
Favorites of Today

We've looked at what we sponge up, what we pay attention to, and what our childhoods were like. Our last stop is to take a look at our current interests, passions, influences, and obsessions.

1. Think of a subject that is important to you in your life. It could be something big, like your family or career. Or it could be something small, like food or movies.

2. Open your sketchbook to the next blank page and with your pencil, write the name of your subject at the top of the page, and then draw 10 circles on the page as big as can fit. No worries if they end up in different sizes.

3. Now with whichever pen you like, draw 10 drawings within those circles representing 10 of your favorite things within that subject.

For example, if you chose food as your important subject (I totally did), you could draw your 10 favorite desserts.

Why We Did It

We're getting more drawing practice in, while also taking stock of what we're currently being influenced by and thinking about.

ASSIGNMENT 6.4
Things to Draw

Have you ever sat down to draw and then your mind immediately went blank? Maybe you tried the spiral exercise and alphabet exercise from earlier, but still... nothing! Let's solve that problem.

1. Turn to the next page in your sketchbook and with your fineliner pen, make a list numbered 1–50, two columns of 25.

2. Write down as many things you like to draw as you can think of. Only write it down if you *actually* enjoy or want to draw it, not if it's something you think you *should* draw.

It could be something specific like vintage stamps, or it could be broader like mechanical things. Do you like drawing animals? What kind? What about cars? People? Girls? Boys? Mountains? Sci-fi? Fantasy? Flowers? Patterns?

You don't have to fill out the whole list right now. Just write the ones that easily come to mind. As time goes on, and you think of or discover more things you enjoy drawing, come back and add them to the list!

Why We Did It

We all have things we're drawn to (pun!), that we keep coming back to or feel the urge to draw again and again. These things can be a great springboard for more drawings. Don't ignore what you're attracted to—follow it!

In the future, if you sit down to draw and feel blocked, come back to this list, and start drawing one of the things you know you love drawing. This is a great way to get your hand moving. From there the lines will probably keep flowing. Now you've got a drawing jump starter!

Paying Attention

What We Notice

Drawing is a great way to be present and pay attention to everything around us. As artists, we have to learn to notice and reflect on the world around us.

But we also need to learn to pay attention to what we pay attention to. We need to keep track of the things we notice. And our sketchbook is a great way to do that.

We can think of our sketchbook as a place to collect pieces of our day-to-day life. After a while, these pieces will begin to repeat and form patterns. And those patterns can then give us a key to unlock what goes on in our subconscious—if we pay attention.

If we see, hear, and reflect on the world around us, keeping track of those pieces from our days, and then pay attention to and notice the patterns that emerge, our sketchbook will become a treasure map. A map full of clues on what we gravitate towards naturally, which can inform and inspire our art, voice, and style.

ASSIGNMENT 6.5a
Influences Today

This is a two-part assignment. Feel free to split up the parts if you don't have enough time for both right now.

1. Turn your sketchbook horizontal, and with your fineliner pen, divide the page into 7 columns, with one row at the top, like this:

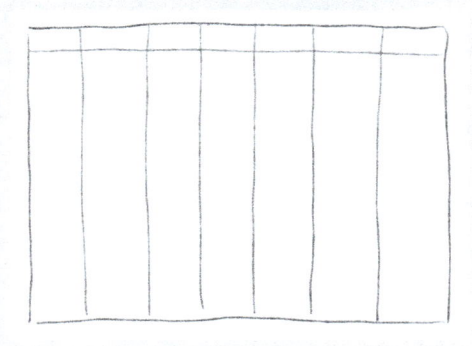

2. Write the following category names at the top of each column:

- Movies
- Books
- TV shows
- Artists
- Bands/Musicians
- Writers
- *Free Space* (add a category you love that I left out!

3. Fill in the columns with all your favorite forms of art media!

Do this before moving on to the second part of this assignment!

Chapter 6: Discovering Our Ideas

ASSIGNMENT 6.5b
Influences Today

1. On the next page, draw two perpendicular arrows across the whole page, dividing the page into four equal sections, like a graph.

2. Label the top of the page *Academic*, the right side *Serious*, the bottom *Entertaining*, and the left side *Playful*.

3. Look back at the list of favorites you made in the first part of this assignment, and pick one category. Plot each favorite from that category on this graph where you think it belongs. Something like this, but with more plots:

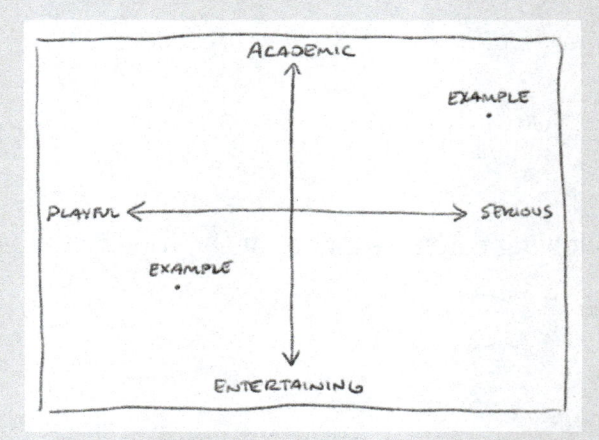

Why We Did It

I think one of the most powerful things you can know about yourself as an artist is who and what your artistic influences are. We made a list of our favorite things as kids and now we've made a list of our current favorite things.

Some of your favorite things as a kid might still be your favorite things now and that's totally fine! One of my favorite movies now is the same movie that was my favorite when I was young (My Neighbor Totoro!). No shame there.

The graph from part two of this assignment helps give us a visual representation of what kind of art influences us most. Think about what this might mean about your own work. Not everyone enjoys making the same kinds of art they enjoy experiencing, but I'll bet there's a strong correlation between what you like and what you make. It might be interesting to keep this chart in mind as you work on developing your style and voice.

Chapter 6: Discovering Our Ideas

ASSIGNMENT 6.6
Reflect on your day in your sketchbook.

Heads up! You'll actually be drawing this assignment tomorrow. But read through the instructions now, so you can pay attention and be prepared for it tomorrow.

1. Starting tomorrow at whatever time choose, use your fineliner pen to divide your sketchbook page into four sections. Write the date at the top of the page.

2. Now let's label our boxes.

- First box: *Things I Did* and a numbered list 1-5
- Second box: *Things I Saw* and a numbered list 1-5
- Third box: *Things I Heard* and a numbered list 1-3
- Fourth box: *Something I Saw* and leave it empty

It should look something like this:

68

3. Inside those boxes, reflect on the day you had yesterday. First, write down 5 things you did.

5. Then write down 5 things you saw.

6. Write down 3 things you heard.

7. And lastly, draw one thing you saw. The thing you draw can be one of the things you listed in the *Things I Saw* box or something else you saw yesterday. Draw however you want, with whatever tool you'd like!

Why We Did It

You may have struggled at first to think of and remember all these things. Or you may think your answers are boring. That's ok! As this book goes on, we'll be learning to pay more attention and be more aware of what goes on around us.

You knew ahead of time that you were going to record parts of your day the next with this assignment. Hopefully, this helped you pay more attention to the world around you during the day. Try to keep this awareness going forward. Start noticing what you notice. What you do each day. What other people say. What other people do. It's all fuel for our art.

Chapter 6: Discovering Our Ideas

Ideas Come from Actions

How Do We Find Ideas?

We've talked about ideas coming from our interests, our passions, the things we notice, our daily life, and our childhood memories. But we don't always go around noticing all the ideas that surround us.

So how do we find ideas? Where do the ideas come from?

Ideas come from action. They come from drawing.

Creating a drawing and creating an idea are so intertwined it's often hard to separate them. Sometimes you'll start a drawing already with an idea. The idea leads you to draw. But we can't wait on or depend on that to happen. We have to be creating more regularly than that to grow and improve and keep up our creative and drawing muscles.

So even when we don't have an idea, we should still draw. And that act of drawing will bring ideas to us. It will cause new thoughts, ideas, and connections to be made in your brain that you wouldn't have thought of if you hadn't just started drawing. It sounds paradoxical, but starting without an idea will lead you to an idea.

Remember, what Picasso said: "Inspiration exists, but it has to find you working."

Chapter 6: Discovering Our Ideas

ASSIGNMENT 6.7
Make a Picture Word Map

1. Turn to the next blank page, and with your fineliner or brush pen, draw a circle in the middle of the page. Now write the name of a noun in that circle. Write it small, at the bottom of the circle, leaving some room inside.

It can be anything that's interested you recently. Try to think back to the things you've been noticing, with your new artist-awareness! Is there anything you keep thinking about or keep seeing everywhere? Just write down the first thing that pops into your head.

2. Now draw a quick, 10-second drawing of that thing inside the circle. Don't fuss too much, just draw it real quick and simple.

3. Draw 3 lines coming out of that circle, with a new circle at the end of each line. Outside the first circle, write *Similar*; on the next circle, write *Different*; and on the last circle, write *Physical Traits*. Like this:

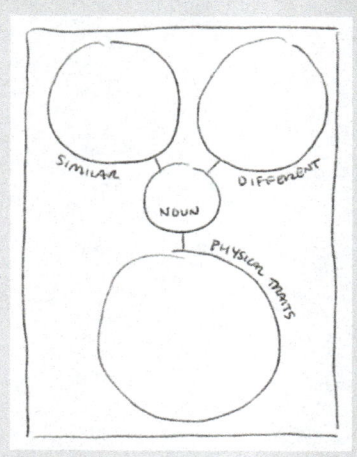

4. Starting with the Synonyms circle, draw something that's similar to your original noun. Keep it small to leave room for multiple drawings. For example, if your noun is "bicycle", you could draw a motorcycle here.

5. Continue in this section, drawing as many similar things as you can think of. You could also draw a tricycle, a moped, a scooter...

6. Once you're done with the Similar circle, move on to the Different circle and do the same. What's different from a bicycle? A car? A bus? Walking? Draw as many as you can think of.

7. In the last circle, draw all the physical traits of your original noun you can think of. Some of them might be hard to represent in a drawing, but do your best and think abstractly with the goals of simplicity and clarity. For bicycle, you could draw, metal, shiny, hard, rubbery... draw as many as you can!

Why We Did It

This assignment helps us learn to visually brainstorm and encourages us to make new connections and come up with original ideas.

Making a picture word map is a great exercise if you have a concept you think might take you somewhere interesting and want to follow it deeper. Try it out again if you're stuck on an idea and don't know where to go next with it!

EXPIRED!
WHAT DID YOU SAY?
WHY
WILD BUG APPEARED!
BELIEVE!
EDWARD LEE
FOOD
PLATE.
AUTHENTIC
CHEF & AUTHOR
SOUP
EXPERIENCES
FINISHED.
WHAT MAKES US AMERICAN?
DIVERSITY
LEARNING
ART
GOODBYE
ATLANTA

CHAPTER 7

Exploring Our Voice

Drawing is About Seeing

Seeing the Essence of Things

Most people assume learning to draw well is about learning to physically draw well. They believe if they can just learn how to move the pencil correctly with their hands, how to make the pen do what they want it to do, then they'll finally be able to draw well.

But the key to drawing something you're proud of, happy with, and feel is drawn in your own style, is much deeper than how you move your hands.

It's instead about how you see the world. What do you notice, what do you recognize as important? Can you see the essence of something, the thing as a whole, not just its parts? And then can you choose what to keep and what to leave out, when you draw that thing so the essence is clear?

That's what makes someone good at drawing or not.

I've heard from so many people "Oh I can't draw", and when I reply, "Actually I think you can" their reasoning is usually that artists just see the world differently than other people.

And yes! I agree, that's absolutely true. But that in no way means you can't also see the world the way artists do.

You can learn to see the world for what it is, you can see the beauty that others overlook, you can recognize the wonderful uniqueness and depth of everything around you. You can observe the world around you, break it down and then make art from it.

The way you think isn't set in stone. And your skills aren't set in stone. You are an individual person, and you can change, grow and improve to be and do whatever it is you want to do.

As long as... you do the work.

ASSIGNMENT 7.1
Minute Drawings

1. Using a light-colored marker, draw 6 large circles on the page and color them in.

2. Now, using the pen of your choice, draw 6 things that are sitting near you right now on top of those 6 circles. Don't overthink which things to draw, it doesn't matter what you pick. Just pick 6 things! It could be a glass of water, your dog, a pen, or anything!

Take just 1-2 minutes per drawing, trying to capture the overall shape and a few basic details about the thing.

Why We Did It

This assignment eases us into observational drawing (drawing what we see) helping us learn to observe and break things down to draw them.

Chapter 7: Exploring Our Voice

ASSIGNMENT 7.2
Draw contours

Now we're going to practice *Contour Drawing*. The word Contour means "outline" in French, and this type of drawing is just that: outline drawing. So let's try it out!

1. Turn to the next blank page in your sketchbook and get out your fineliner or brush pen.

2. Sit down wherever you normally draw. We're going to draw a contour drawing of the desk or table or whatever you're drawing on right now. You can start this by beginning to draw the edges of the objects on the desk. Start your line at one point on the page, and slowly continue drawing the same line, not lifting the pen, looking up at the desk, and "tracing" the edges of the desk and objects.

Try to see the desk and things as one object, and trace the contour of that big object. Just draw what's right in front of you, no need to draw things you can't see, like the legs beneath the table.

Go slow, and take your time. Don't make sketchy lines, make one smooth, continuous line. Be sure to keep looking back up at the desk as you're drawing.

And that's it! You've made a contour drawing!

Why We Did It

Making contour drawings helps us focus on the overall shape of an object, rather than getting caught up in the details. It's also a great way to strengthen our spatial skills, by observing the spacing of objects we see and practicing how to record that spacing on the page.

ASSIGNMENT 7.3
Draw a more complex contour drawing

1. Grab a chair, your timer, your sketchbook, and your fineliner or brush pen and head to the kitchen or cooking area in your home.

2. Sit down in the chair as far back from the kitchen as you can while being able to see the entire room or as much of it as you can.

3. Set your timer for 10 minutes and hit start. Using your pen, draw the contour of your kitchen. It seems impossible, I know! It's a big space and there's a lot of stuff in there. But remember, try to see the whole kitchen as one big shape, and focus on the outline of that shape. Forget the drawers on the cabinets, the door to the stove, or the tiles on the wall. Focus on outlining one big shape right from where you're sitting.

4. Now, draw lines inside the contour drawing, breaking the shape down into parts of the kitchen. Start with the big parts, like drawing a line to form the oven, or drawing a line to form the refrigerator. Then move on to the smaller parts, drawing lines for the separate drawers, or canisters holding utensils.

5. Keep going, getting more and more detailed until your 10 minutes runs out. Looks pretty interesting, huh?

Why We Did It

Like our last contour drawings, this assignment helps us focus on the overall shape of an object, rather than getting caught up in the details. This is a helpful technique when attempting to draw something complex—like an entire kitchen! It would be overwhelming to start with the details. Starting with a contour allows us to see the overall shape first, planning and setting our composition and spacing on the page.

Drawing from the Heart, then the Brain

Drawing from the Heart

Many people begin their art journey by trying to draw things "correctly". By trying to represent things in their drawings—to draw things exactly how they see them.

But this is only one way to draw, not the only way, or the best way, in my opinion.

To me, it's more interesting to not worry about drawing things "correctly" and instead draw from your heart. Draw how you feel. Draw your *interpretation* of the things you see, not the representation.

Don't worry about what's good or bad, right or wrong. Just draw what comes to you. Draw because you enjoy drawing. Draw what you like and draw what sparks your curiosity.

Draw This, Not That

There's a wonderful book, *Drawn to Life: 20 Golden Years of Disney Master Classes: Volume 1: The Walt Stanchfield Lectures*. If you've taken any of my online classes, you've heard me probably talk your ear off about this book.

Stanchfield was an animator at Walt Disney Studios and worked on films including *The Jungle Book* and *The Aristocats*. He led an animator training class series at Disney Studios where he taught our current animator celebrities like Brad Bird and John Lasseter. A bunch of his lectures were written down and compiled into this book along with hundreds of his sketches.

My favorite and most helpful tip from Stanchfield is something he states over and over in the book: "draw gesture, not anatomy." And he repeats this concept in many different ways:

- Draw the whole pose, not body parts
- Draw verbs (actions), not nouns
- Draw ideas (story), not drawings (things)

Basically, when you're sketching an action (ie. a person lifting a heavy object), you want to focus on that overall concept and not on how to draw their button-down shirt or hair or fingers. You want to keep your drawings simple when you're first beginning a drawing and get down the overall pose and action before diving into all the fun details. If the base of your drawing isn't successful, all the amazing and unique details in the world won't be able to save it.

Focusing on the gesture and action helps bring vitality and life into your final drawing.

Think of it this way: You aren't drawing a button-down shirt worn by a person lifting a board, you're drawing a person lifting a board, who happens to be wearing a button-down shirt, happens to have hair, and happens to have fingers.

So in the beginning stages of drawing, try to focus on drawing the *energy* of the action happening, rather than the individual body parts attached to a body.

Chapter 7: Exploring Our Voice

ASSIGNMENT 7.4
Draw a chart of emotions

1. Open your sketchbook to the next blank page, and using your fineliner pen, draw two arrows across the page, dividing the page up into four equal sections, like a graph.

2. Now draw 12 circles on the page, placing three in each quadrant. The size, exact placement, and spacing aren't important. Make it random, spread them out, and switch it up! I'm not going to show you an example, so as not to influence you. Draw them however you like.

3. At the intersection of the two arrows, write the label, *Neutral*.

- Label the end of the arrow pointing up, *Excited*
- Label the end of the arrow pointing right, *Happy*
- Label the end of the arrow pointing down, *Calm*
- Label the end of the arrow pointing left, *Angry*

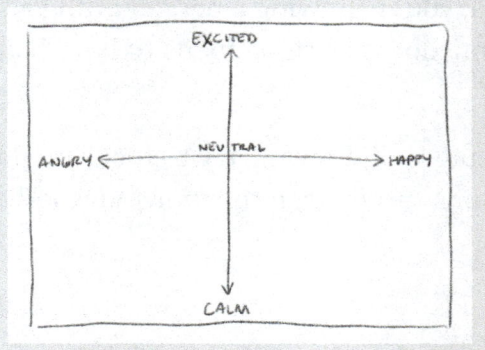

4 Now imagine each circle on this graph as a face. Draw facial features on the faces to represent where they fall on the graph of emotions. For example, a face all the way to the left of the page would be very angry.

Keep your drawings quick and simple, just two eyes, a nose, and a mouth, and maybe some eyebrows. Think about how to convey emotion through facial expressions. Think about what your eyes do when you're angry. How do you shape your mouth when you're sad?

You can use some extra details to communicate the emotion—like puffs, tears, or veins—but don't go crazy or rely too much on them. Try to communicate as much as you can with just the facial features.

Why We Did It

Exploration, baby! We're experimenting to discover how *you* like to draw faces and emotions.

Chapter 7: Exploring Our Voice

Assignment 7.5

Draw a page full of everyday events

Step 1: Grab your timer again, and using your fineliner pen, divide the next page into 20 sections, 4x5.

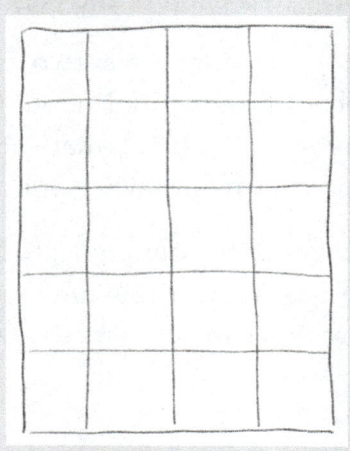

Step 2: We're going to draw some simple everyday events in time intervals. Set your timer to 30 seconds and draw your interpretation of each of the following prompts, each for 30 seconds only.

It could be a literal representation, an experience you had with the event, a symbol, an icon, a piece of clothing, food—just draw the first thing you think of! Remember to keep it simple!

Ready? Set your timer for 30 seconds, hit start, look at the list on the next page, and draw!

A birthday	Office meeting
Homework time	Travel day
Wedding day	Tax day
Date night	Road trip
Hair appointment	Sports event
Movie night	Walking the dog
Lunchtime	Gym time
Phone call	Feeding the cat
Grocery shopping	Commuting to work

Why We Did It

Like the interval assignments before, drawing with a time constraint forces you to loosen up and draw without overthinking. We're also beginning to explore and expand the types of things we're drawing.

Chapter 7: Exploring Our Voice

ASSIGNMENT 7.6
Drawing different views

1. Turn to the next page and using your fineliner pen, divide the page into 16 sections, 4x4.

2. Choose 4 things that happen to be around you right now and label each box in the first column with one of the four things. It could be anything—your cat, a lamp, a coffee mug... just pick four things. Something like this:

3. Now, draw each thing in the box you labeled. Don't spend forever on this, you've only got a small space to work with on purpose! Something kinda like this:

4. Now we're going to draw across the rows. I want you to draw the same thing three more times across the row. So in this example, my top row will have pizza drawn 4 different times. *But here's the catch!* For each new version, draw that thing from a different angle. A different view of the same thing.

My first drawing was a slice of pizza from above, so my second could be from the side, my third from 3/4 view, and my fourth from the bottom!

Have fun!

Why We Did It

This assignment helps us start exploring drawing things in different ways, and expanding the way we think, to go beyond our initial ideas and thoughts. We're also practicing drawing different points of view. Multitasking, y'all.

Worrying What Others Will Think

Fear of How Our Art Is Received

We often worry about what other people will think about what we make. We worry they won't like it. We worry they'll think it's bad. But we can't let that stop us from making art.

There are a few reasons why someone might not understand or like your artwork:

1. It's just not their thing.
2. They saw the art too early in the process and it hasn't worked through all its kinks yet.
3. That person just ain't ready for you.

Which artists are who history remembers most: the artists who followed the rules and did what everyone liked? Or the artists who did what felt right to them, broke all the rules, and made up their own rules? How many artists had their work ridiculed and mocked at first, but then celebrated as revolutionary and innovative later?

No matter what the reason is that someone doesn't like your work, it doesn't matter. Don't let the power of your artmaking fall to other people's approval. Your art is *your* art, and only *you* know how to make it.

All that matters is that you keep going and keep making more art.

ASSIGNMENT 7.7
Draw a step-by-step recipe

On the next page in your sketchbook, using your black pen and one extra color, draw a recipe for one of your favorite foods.

You can choose a complicated family recipe, or something as simple as a bowl of cereal. You can use a recipe you know by heart, or look one up.

Write out the instructions and draw the steps of the recipe, illustrating the ingredients and actions. Fit the recipe on one page and remember to include the title of the recipe!

Why We Did It

This assignment helps us learn to space elements out on a page in our minds. Being able to estimate compositions in our drawings takes practice, but we're working our way there!

We're also pushing further with open-ended assignments, and beginning to explore adding color to our work.

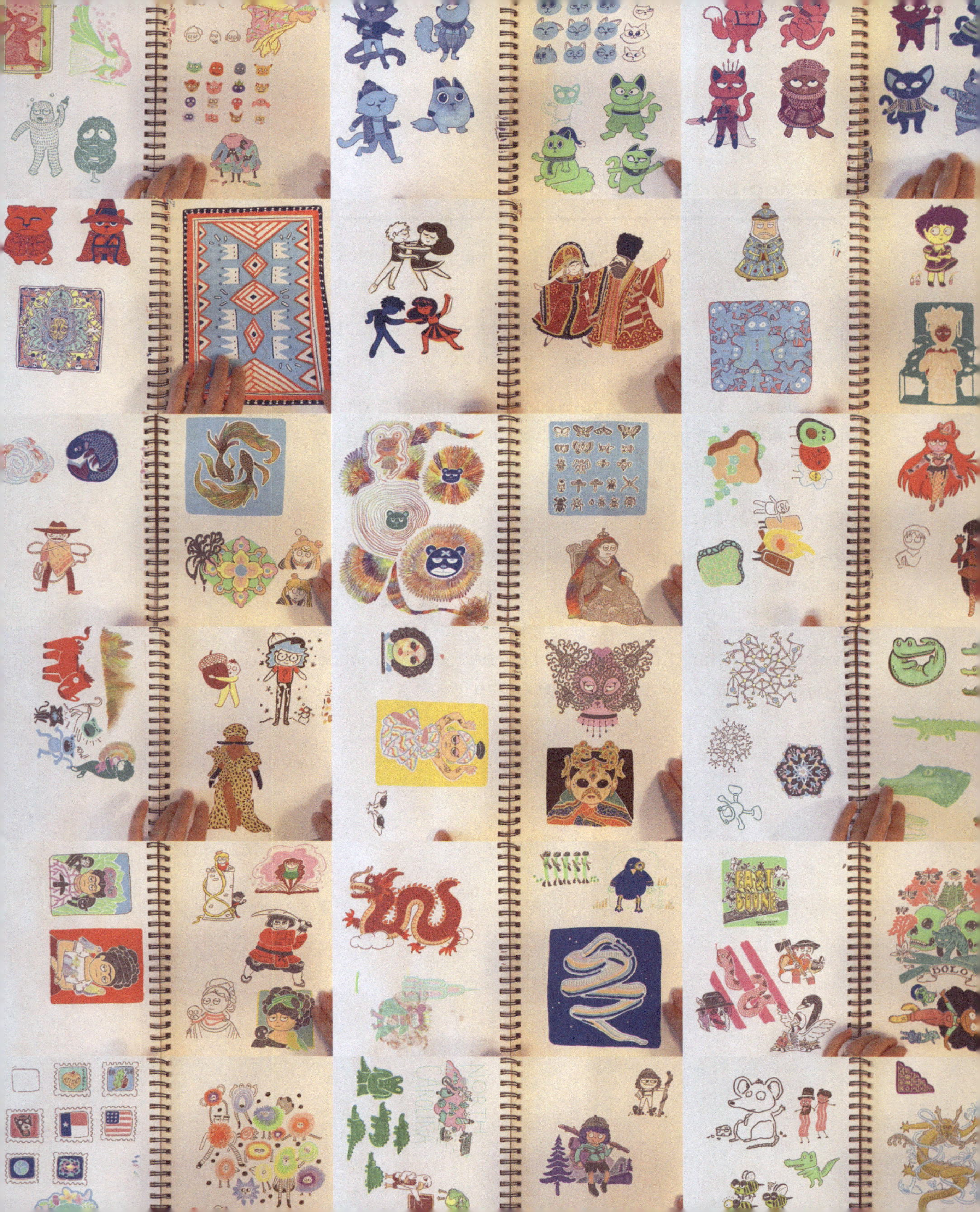

CHAPTER 8
Experimenting with Ways of Drawing

Representation vs. Interpretation

When I'm drawing something that actually exists in front of me—meaning I'm not drawing something made up or imaginary—I like to begin sketching semi-realistically. I don't ever draw in a photorealistic style (that just ain't me), but if I'm drawing, say, a bug on my kitchen floor, I'll start out trying to draw it as I see it.

Drawings at this stage are a great way to learn about the thing: how it looks, how it moves, even how it sounds can be important. We're observing it and recording it by drawing it.

Drawing the representation of reality is called Mimesis. Realism and photorealism are examples of styles of mimesis.

You're certainly welcome to draw photorealistically. But in my personal opinion, your art could be so much stronger if you didn't stop there and instead went deeper than just representing the reality you see. The technical skill is impressive, but where's the vitality, life, and uniqueness?

Instead, you could draw your *interpretation* of reality. This taps into not only the reality but also the way *you* see it. It includes your expression of self, your communication of feelings, and your unique voice. Those are the things that elevate a drawing into a piece of art with a unique style.

So when you're drawing from life, once you've drawn the thing a few times and you feel like you have a good understanding of it, you can then begin to step a bit away from reality. This is where you're able to inject your personality by interpreting what you've learned about the thing from drawing and observing it.

You can now start to embellish your drawings, not drawing directly from the thing, trying to represent it as it physically is, but instead drawing your interpretation of it, trying to draw the essence of the thing, the way you feel that it is.

ASSIGNMENT 8.1
Draw a page of famous artists

1. Turn to the next page in your sketchbook and using your fineliner pen, divide the page into 12 sections, a 3x4 grid.

2. Write the following names small at the bottom of each section, making a box around the name:

    Salvador Dali   Frida Kahlo

    David Bowie   Jimi Hendrix

    Henri Matisse   Andy Warhol

    Haruki Murakami   Georgia O'Keefe

    Billie Holiday   Virginia Woolf

    Jackson Pollock   Claude Monet

3. Now, on your computer or phone, search for each artist and find a photo of them you like. Don't spend too long looking, just pick one!

4. In each box, using your reference image, draw a portrait of that artist, with whatever drawing tool you like. Draw the head and shoulders only, like a painted portrait. Use whatever drawing tools you like. Be instinctual, make mistakes, and just go for it! Try to capture the *essence* of the person, not a direct representation. Include their hairstyle, clothing, facial expression... what makes them unique? Simplify, abstract, exaggerate!

Why We Did It

This assignment helps us practice drawing without trying to get a perfect representation of something. We're not aiming for photorealistic perfection, we're aiming for drawing something in our own way.

Chapter 8: Experimenting with Ways of Drawing

ASSIGNMENT 8.2
Draw a page of famous architecture

1. Turn to the next page in your sketchbook, turn your book horizontal, and using your fineliner pen, divide the page into 9 sections, 3x3, like this:

2. Now write the following names of famous architectural buildings small at the bottom of each section, making a box around the name:

- Taj Mahal
- Sydney Opera House
- Hagia Sophia
- Leaning Tower of Pisa
- Eiffel Tower
- Chrysler Building
- Fallingwater
- St. Basil's Cathedral
- Lotus Temple

3. Now, on your computer or phone, search for each piece of architecture and find a photo of them you like. Like before, don't spend too long looking, just pick one!

4. In each box, use your reference and draw that building! Get the overall shape down first. You can add as many details as you like, but remember, you don't have to include everything! Try to capture the *essence* of the architecture, not a direct representation.

Why We Did It

Like the last assignment, we're amping it up and drawing more complex things in our own way, not worrying about perfect representation or how we think we *should* draw it.

Injecting Personality

So how do you begin to step away from reality and start drawing reality with your personal spin on it? Try a few of these techniques.

Avoid Evenness

Did you know that lines don't have to be straight in your drawings? And repeated parts don't need to be perfectly aligned or perfectly the same! Avoiding evenness when drawing adds interest and often feels more lively and vibrant than if we drew it all with a ruler and t-square.

It may seem counter-intuitive, but imperfections make a drawing feel more real.

Physiognomy

There's a term called Physiognomy which the animator Walt Stanchfield defines as: "the art of discovering temperament and character from outward appearance, hence inner character as revealed outwardly."

This is what we're trying to achieve in our observational drawings now. You understand the subject and you've drawn it pretty accurately, now you need to start pulling out its character and emphasizing its personality by embellishing and stepping away from actuality.

Push your drawings farther than reality. Draw that bug bigger than it actually is, make its eyes huge to add some humanity and cuteness—you can even make it smile if you want to!

Or take it the other direction if the bug gives you a different feeling: draw the bug with tiny menacing eyes, long spindly legs, and matted hair.

Focus on your interpretation of the thing, and its temperament you feel, rather than just the generic label of "bug" your brain applies to all insects.

Chapter 8: Experimenting with Ways of Drawing

Your brain only sees the bug as an animal with six legs and antennae. But your heart sees the bug as more than that—your heart knows how it makes you feel. And *that* is what we want to capture in our art.

Keep One Foot in Reality

Although our goal is to push our art, we also need to keep one foot in reality. We want to push our drawings beyond reality, but still have it somewhat based on the thing itself.

Push your drawings as far as you can, but realize you may have to scale them back again to maintain successful communication and avoid going overboard. We're not trying to draw over-the-top amusement park caricatures here. We're trying to find the true essence of the thing we're drawing.

So take a step back every now and then to make sure you haven't gone too far!

ASSIGNMENT 8.3
Draw a moving, living thing

---

1. Choose a person or animal who lives in your home, or visits your home frequently.

2. Spend a few minutes observing that person/animal doing something, whether it be cooking, sleeping, walking, chewing on a bone… whatever they happen to be doing when you sit down to observe.

3. Then begin drawing them in your sketchbook with the tool of your choice. Keep your drawings quick and loose—they're going to be moving, so you've got to move fast!

If you can help it, don't let them know you're drawing, or tell them to ignore you. Don't ask them to pause or hold a pose. Try to capture things as they naturally happen.

Try to capture the feel of what they're doing and how they're behaving. Do they seem stressed? Are they hurrying? Do they seem relaxed? Happy? Get as much of their essence on the page as you can, and fill up the page with drawings.

Why We Did It

This assignment encourages us to observe and draw what we see while also abstracting the person or animal to get to its essence. When we're drawing something moving, we're not able to fuss over the anatomy, pose, or details. Instead, we have to focus on getting down only the parts necessary to communicate who or what it is.

Chapter 8: Experimenting with Ways of Drawing

ASSIGNMENT 8.4
Draw a page full of actions

1. Grab your timer and set it to 30 seconds.

2. Press start on your timer and using your fineliner or brush pen, draw the following actions, one at a time, each for 30 seconds only.

Keep it small and simple and remember to focus on the action, not the details. Don't worry about drawing anatomy—focus on the gesture.

Ready? Set your timer for 30 seconds, press start, and go!

Shouting	Jumping
Sitting	Standing w/ arms crossed
Kneeling	Eating
Swaying	Running
Doing yoga	Shooting a basketball
Swimming	Stretching
Yelling	Singing
Dancing	Sleeping

Why We Did It

Like the interval assignments before, drawing with a time constraint forces you to loosen up and draw without overthinking and worrying about anatomy and body parts. Don't worry if your actions don't quite look like what you intended. That's ok! It's all practice and this was your first time doing this!

Abstract to Emphasize

Abstracting a Thing to its Essential Elements

Another good way to step away from reality is to abstract the subject. To abstract something is to reduce it down to only the essential elements. You want to drop a majority of the detail out, leaving only the necessary and most indispensable parts.

If you feel stuck, try describing your concept in words and write it down in your sketchbook. For example, say I'm going to draw a bug crawling across my desk. (I guess I've been noticing a lot of bugs lately?) I would write down:

> *There is a bug crawling across my desk.*

Then add some adverbs. So I would write:

> *There is a bug **hurriedly** crawling across my desk.*

Now we've got a little extra boost to inspire some personality and story in our drawing! Drawing adverbs tells how the action is happening and hints at why it's happening. This creates a story, and remember: we're aiming to draw actions and stories and feelings, not just dull, exact replicas of things. We've got cameras for that. We're here to draw.

Chapter 8: Experimenting with Ways of Drawing

ASSIGNMENT 8.5
Draw a collection of things

1. Pick a non-moving thing that you have a bunch of in your home. It could be coffee mugs, books, or bottles of hot sauce—anything that has variety within the same category!

2. Collect a group of them together—at least 5 and no more than 10.

3. Spread the collection out on your desk or table and open your sketchbook to the next blank page.

4. Using your fineliner or brush pen, draw each of those things on the page. Try to draw the things as they are, as you really see them. But as you draw each thing, think about the differences between them. Do they feel different? Do they have different moods, different feels, or different memories?

5. Label each drawing, and write down notes about each thing. How does that thing make you feel? Do you like it more than the others? Less than the others? Is it older? Newer? Cleaner? Dirtier? Do you remember when, where, and how you got it? Fill the page with drawings and notes.

Why We Did It

This assignment encourages us to focus on drawing our interpretation of things, rather than the representation of things. We're practicing putting our own spin on it and injecting our personality into our work.

Sketchbook to Style

3 Basic Drawing Guidelines

You guys are getting pretty advanced in your drawing skills! I think you're ready to handle a few drawing guidelines. Remember though, there are no rules in art. Break these guidelines if you want, ignore them if you want. They're just tips that have helped me and may help you.

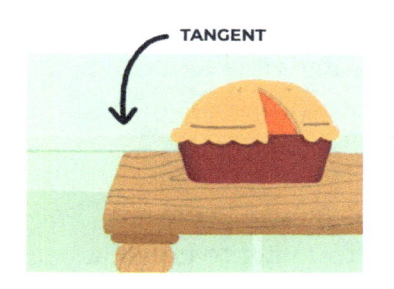

1. Avoid tangent lines.

A tangent is when two lines come together to make an unintended relationship. Here you can see a line in the background runs into a line on the table, which destroys the depth of the picture.

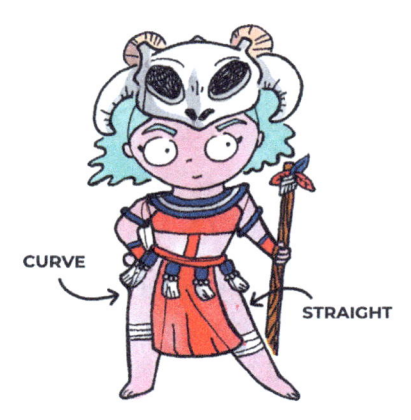

2. Use straights against curves.

Contrasting straight lines against curved lines helps create depth and interest.

3. Overlap elements.

Overlapping one thing in front of another creates depth by adding layers to your work.

101

Chapter 8: Experimenting with Ways of Drawing

ASSIGNMENT 8.6
Recreate a favorite piece of art

1. Choose one of your favorite pieces of art. It could be a painting by a classical artist, a cartoon by a favorite illustrator, a scene from a favorite animator, or a page from a comic by your favorite comic author. Whatever you like—choose what comes to your mind quickly!

2. Find an image of that piece of art online. Take some time to look at the piece of art. Think about why the piece of art is special to you and what you like about it.

3. Now open your sketchbook to the next blank page, and using whichever tool you prefer, redraw the piece of art. Do **not** to create a direct replica and definitely don't trace it! Redraw it in your own way.

4. When you're done, be sure to write a caption at the bottom or top of the page naming the artist and title of the piece if there is one, so you remember later what you copied.

Why We Did It

Copying can be a great way to learn why we like a certain piece of art and to learn how to implement some of its elements into our own work. We can discover what makes the piece work, and how to merge elements from other art with our art to make new, original art.

I hope this is obvious without me saying, but you should never copy another artist's work and try to pass it off as your own. Copying can be a great way to learn, and I certainly copied a lot of Pokemon and Sailor Moon when I was first learning to draw. But if you share copied work, you need to be honest and state that it's a copy. Give the credit to the original artist, preferably linking to them if you're sharing online.

Combining Words + Pictures

Comics are a great to combine words and pictures in drawing. Comics have multiple different uses for words and are written differently than a novel or other non-illustrated story would be. Here are some different ways comics use words to tell a graphic story:

Dialogue

Text in speech bubbles

Narration

A third-person omniscient point of view

Sound effects

Onomatopoeia like BANG, DING, or POW

Chapter 8: Experimenting with Ways of Drawing

Tips for When to Use Words or Not

So if we're open to using words with our drawings, how should we decide when to include them? When should we just draw something, and when should we draw something *and* include words? Here are some tips for deciding whether to use words or not when you're drawing:

Show, don't tell.

If you can show something with pictures, rather than words, it's generally best in comics to use pictures. Instead of having your character say, "I feel sad", instead you can *show* they are sad. Is he crying? Is his head hung down? Is he wallowing on the couch?

Keep your bubble word count under 30 words.

This is a guideline, not a rule, and it can certainly be broken. But it's a good max count to keep in mind and encourages editing. After 30 words, your bubble will probably start to take over the whole panel!

Word + Picture Combinations

Now let's look at how words and pictures can work together to communicate one message. In Scott McCloud's book, *Making Comics*, which I highly recommend all artists to read, McCloud lays out five ways words and pictures can be combined.

Your comic will be stronger if you allow the words and pictures to work together to tell the story, rather than one telling the story and the other just repeating what was said. These five combos help do just that!

Word Specific

The words tell you everything you need to know, while the pictures highlight part of what's being said.

Picture Specific

The pictures tell you everything you need to know, while the words highlight part of what's being said.

Duo Specific

The words and pictures pretty much say the same thing.

Intersecting

The words and pictures help communicate the same message, each saying something new the other didn't say.

Interdependent

The words and pictures work together to say something that neither could say alone.

Chapter 8: Experimenting with Ways of Drawing

ASSIGNMENT 8.7
Draw a one-page comic about the seasons

Open your sketchbook to the next blank page, and draw a one-page comic about the four seasons: Winter, Spring, Summer, and Fall.

Use your black pen and 1-2 additional colors, either a marker or colored pencil, whichever you prefer.

You can plan out your comic a little bit, writing out the story and organizing what will be in the panels beforehand, but do all this process work in your sketchbook too. And don't draw the final comic in pencil first, just go for it in ink!

The story can be narrative with characters, or more abstract and experimental. The number of panels and word use is up to you, but the comic must fit within one page. Try to capture the mood of the seasons in your comic.

Why Comics?

One reason I'm asking you to draw comics is to try to get you thinking about more than one option and exploring more than your first idea. Another reason is that comics are a strong method of storytelling. And as I said before, what we're really aiming to do in this course is uncover *your* story.

Just because we're using comics to try to uncover your art doesn't mean you have to keep making comics in the future, or even that I'm trying to get you to adopt comics as your art form. Comics are just the medium we're using right now to get our thoughts and ideas on the page. Remember, it's about the process, not the final product.

ASSIGNMENT 8.8
Draw a recent conversation as a comic

On the next blank page in your sketchbook, using either your fineliner or brush pen, draw a comic of a conversation you had or overheard recently.

Think back to the tips of when to use words (or not), types of words you can use, and ways to combine words and pictures.

Why We Did It

This assignment lets us practice using words and pictures together, using *Show, Don't Tell*, and the different word + picture combinations we learned about previously.

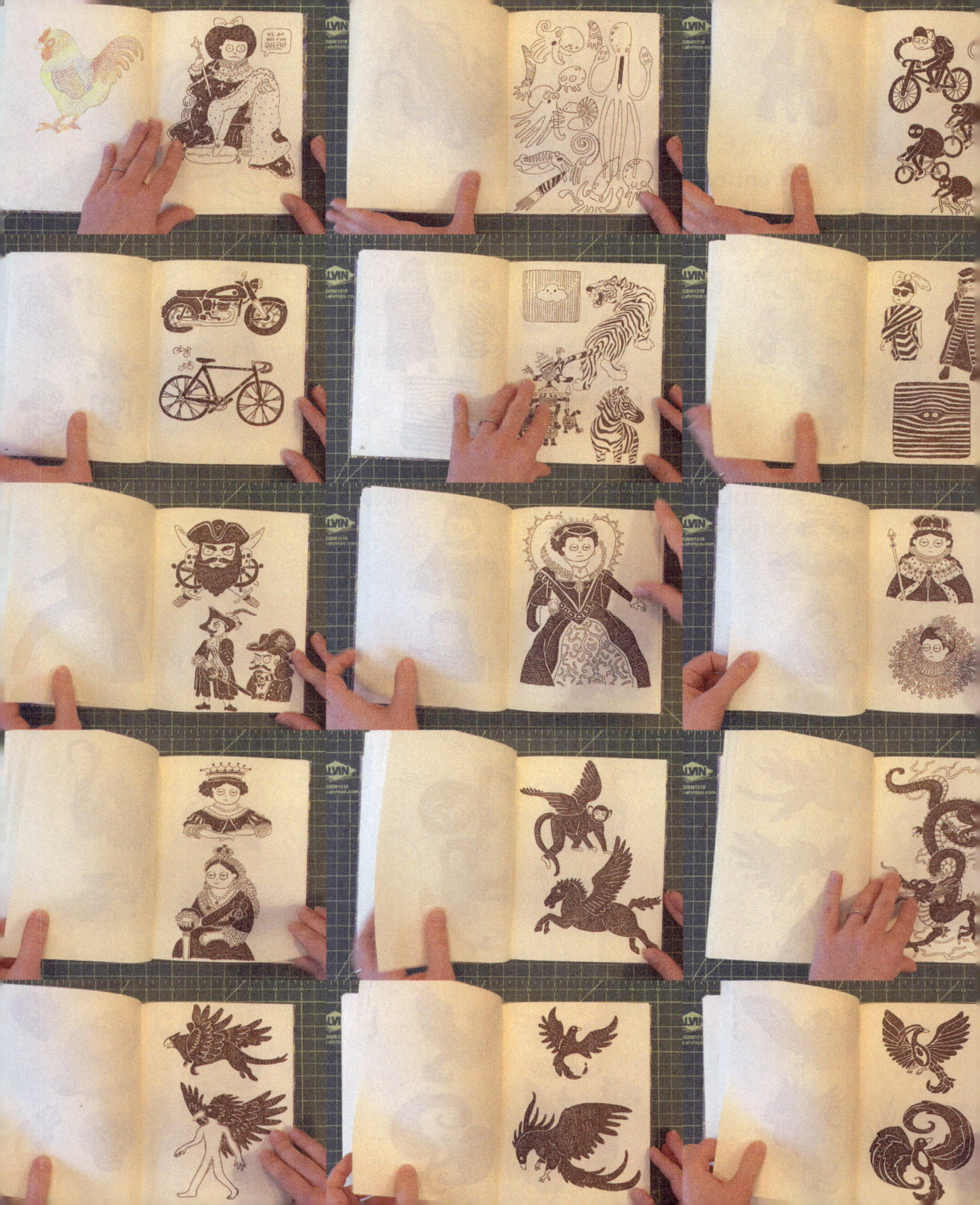
QUEEN?

CHAPTER 9

Refining Our Visual Style

Your Mini-Me

Ok, y'all are ready for the big time now! We're going to draw a self-portrait character, something I like to call your Mini-Me. But we're not breaking out the mirror and going photo-realistic here. We're trying to capture the essence of ourselves, our interpretation of ourselves, not the actual representation of ourselves.

This assignment may feel daunting at first, but try to keep an open mind, have fun, and explore! You don't have to completely finalize your Mini-Me now—we'll be working with and developing your character over the next series of assignments! So don't worry, this is just the start of your Mini-Me!

Drawing yourself is simple in theory, but difficult in practice. Immediately when people see the instructions to draw a self-portrait, drawing "rules" come to mind. You may feel the urge to draw accurate human anatomy and start worrying how you'll draw your nose, your legs, and definitely those dreaded hands!

What's happening is simple—too much thinking. In that frustrating scenario, we began our process of drawing not by drawing, but by thinking. We *think* a human has to look a certain way, and we try to draw it in that predetermined way, instead of allowing ourselves to explore the infinite possibilities of how a human *could* look.

By beginning with too much thinking, we immediately limit our options and potential. We shut off our experimental, playful side, and we fall back into our perfectionist beliefs and traditional drawing rules.

But that's not what this assignment—or this book—is about. I don't want you to create a photo-realistic recreation of yourself. Drawing in that way, allowing our thinking to dictate how we draw, leads to stiff art, hesitant lines, and generic people that don't look like anyone, much less like you.

What I want you to do is turn off your brain. I want you to explore and play. I want you to find that character that feels like you. I want you to let go of the perfectionist thinking and comparison thinking and begin to uncover the Mini-Me that's hidden deep inside you.

This isn't just about drawing a one-off character. The whole book is about finding yourself as an artist, and this assignment is a direct and literal stab at that idea. It's hard, but you can do it.

Remember that you're not going to immediately sit down and draw your finalized Mini-Me. This is a process. Many students move on from this assignment not totally in love with their character, but over the following assignments, they keep drawing the character in different ways, expanding on what works, removing what doesn't, and making changes as they go along.

Through no-pressure exploration, you'll discover which features feel right and make those bigger, bolder, and more important. With patience and experimentation, your character will morph into something real—you'll begin to find yourself on the page.

So keep drawing, keep trying, keep opening your eyes and exploring the possibilities, and slowly, everything will fall into place. Trust in yourself, trust in the process, and just draw.

Now go give your Mini-Me a chance! You can do it!

ASSIGNMENT 9.1
Draw your Mini-Me!

You got this! Remember everything we talked about—keep an open mind, be patient with the process, and you don't have to create your final Mini-Me today.

1. Open up your sketchbook and, using your fineliner pen, start exploring how to draw your Mini-Me.

2. Try to think about what makes you look like you, and play around with emphasizing those things in your drawing explorations.

3. Keep drawing more explorations, filling up as many pages as you need.

If you get stuck, the next section offers more help, but give it a shot on your own first!

Why We Did It

This assignment is another way to push ourselves into thinking more abstractly and simplifying things down to their essence. It's also our first step in exploring our inner identity on the page. Tapping into our identity will help us tap into our style because they're really one and the same.

We're also going to be using this little character in assignments to come. How you draw yourself can definitely evolve over time too, so don't feel restricted to what you've already done. My Mini-Me has changed slowly over time and looks a little different now than it did even just a year ago. Don't be afraid to play with it as we continue on!

Chapter 9: Refining Our Visual Style

Mini-Me Help + Inspiration

Awesome job tackling this tough assignment! If you're feeling a little frustrated, that's totally normal. Sometimes the creative process is frustrating! But you're here putting in the work and that's what counts.

Try to think more deeply about what makes you look like you, and play around with emphasizing those things in your drawing explorations. For example, I'm quite short (5 feet tall, baby!) and I have a big mop of thick, wavy hair, so that's what I exaggerate with my character, simplifying or ignoring almost all other features.

Which characteristics do you think make you look like you? Do you have big eyes? Big cheeks? Are you tall? Short? Lanky? Curvy? We're trying to capture the real you in all your glory!

In the next assignment, keep drawing more versions of your Mini-Me, filling up as many pages as you need. You can add some accessories if you think they're essential in representing you. Maybe you wear glasses? Or maybe you always wear the same pair of earrings? Or maybe, like me, clothes are not that important to you, and you prefer to just draw yourself with no clothes at all!

To help you keep exploring your Mini-Me, I've put together some Mini-Me inspirations. These are illustrators I love who have developed their own little characters for themselves. Some of their characters are pretty whacky—some are even animal alter egos—the possibilities are endless! Take a look at these examples and see if it sparks anything new for you to try with your own Mini-Me!

Take a look at these Mini-Me inspirations under Assignment 9.1b at: *www.might-could.com/sketchbook-to-style-resources/*

ASSIGNMENT 9.1B
Continue exploring your Mini-Me

Keep drawing and evolving your character with anything you were inspired by in the previous section!

If you still feel unhappy with your Mini-Me, that's ok! We're still going to be working on and evolving this character in the upcoming assignments. You're doing great.

Chapter 9: Refining Our Visual Style

The 7 Visual Elements of Style

As we keep developing our Mini-Me, we're going to add in some visual elements of style, so we can explore those too. An artistic style is made up of many things, but there are some key visual art features that make each style look distinctive. I've condensed this down to what I call the 7 *Visual Elements of Style*. I'm going to introduce the elements to you here, and then we'll explore them more in the upcoming assignments.

Linework

Let's kick off with linework! There are two main features of linework, line width and line quality.

Line Width is how thick or thin a line is.

thick line   thin line   no line

Line Quality is how the line is drawn.

consistent line   varied line   broken line

Linework is often determined by the tool you're using. A brush pen will give you a varied line, a 0.7 mm fineliner pen will give you a thick line, and a 0.1 mm fineliner will give you a thin line.

Color

Next, we have color. A consistent color palette is a core feature of a strong artistic style. But there are more possibilities within that consistency than you might think! Let's focus on two features within color, lightness and saturation.

Lightness is how much white or black is in a color.

LIGHTER (more white) — DARKER (more black)

Saturation is the purity or intensity of a color.

DULLER (less saturated) — BRIGHTER (more saturated)

Form Definition

Did you know the shapes and forms inside every piece of art are defined by other art elements? It's true! There are four main ways to define form: **Line**, **Color**, **Texture**, and **Value**.

line   color   texture   value

Graphic work often uses lines to define forms, while more realistic work tends to use value. These techniques can definitely be used in combo with each other too.

Space

Every piece of art also has a pictorial plane. The artwork either embraces the fact that it is 2-D or aims to give the illusion of being 3-D.

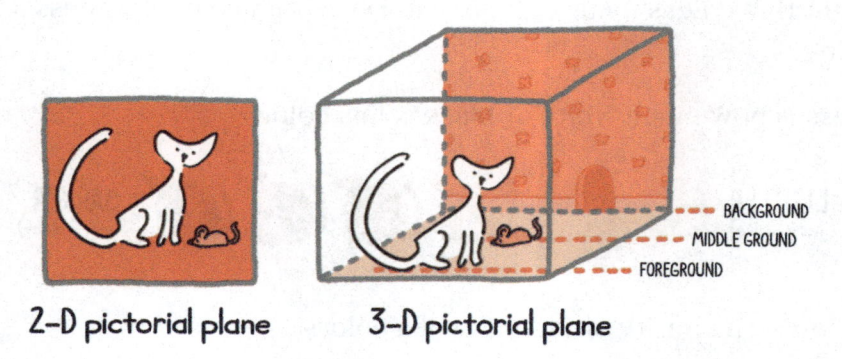

2-D pictorial plane   3-D pictorial plane

BACKGROUND
MIDDLE GROUND
FOREGROUND

The forms in a **2-D Pictorial Plane** live on the same plane, with minimal depth. The forms in a **3-D Pictorial Plane** live on different planes (often a foreground, middle ground, and background) with more realistic depth.

Texture

Texture is another very noticeable and distinctive feature of a style. An artwork's texture is often determined by the tool used. A pencil, alcohol marker, paint pen, or brush pen will each create unique textures. Consistent use of texture is an important part of a strong artistic style.

paint   colored pencil   pen   no texture

Mood

Just like people, artworks go through different moods. But when viewed as a whole, a strong style has a pretty consistent mood. Think of it as the personality of your art. Color is one of the most powerful ways to create moods and evoke emotions. So let's focus on two ways to convey mood in art: Color warmth and color schemes.

Color Warmth: Warmer colors tend to evoke feelings of happiness, hope, or excitement, while cooler colors tend to evoke sadness, despair, or calm.

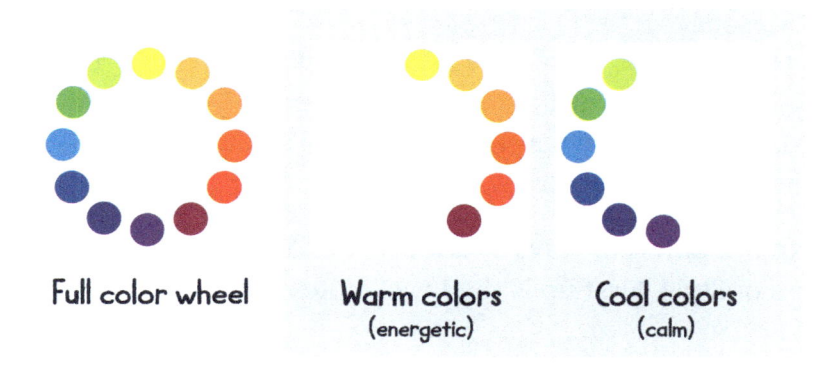

Full color wheel   Warm colors (energetic)   Cool colors (calm)

Color Schemes: Analogous leans pleasant and calm, complementary leans powerful and exciting, triadic leans balanced and confident, and monochromatic leans serene and peaceful.

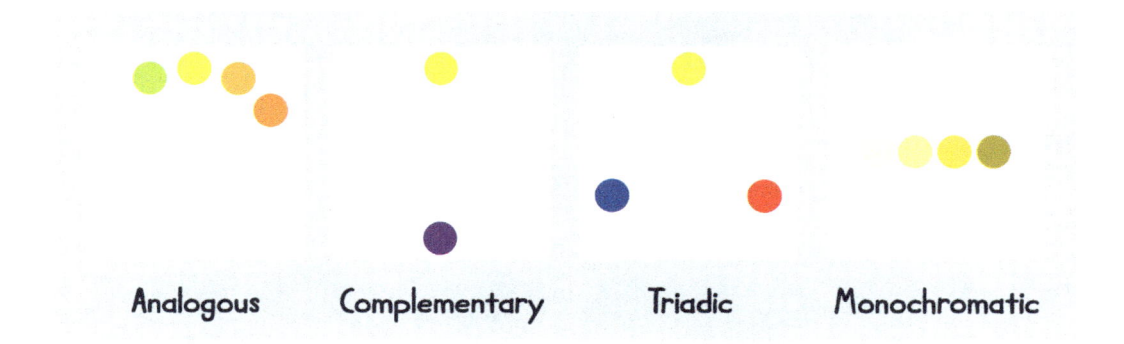

Analogous   Complementary   Triadic   Monochromatic

Chapter 9: Refining Our Visual Style

Level of Realism

Finally, the level of realism you aim for is one of the most defining aspects of your artistic style. This one choice decides (or narrows down) many other stylistic options.

MORE REALISTIC ⟶ MORE ABSTRACT

Keep in mind that there is no "best" level of realism, just like there is no "best" color palette. Every style element is just a matter of your personal taste and what you enjoy drawing. And so, every level of realism has its own merit, from the most realistic to the most abstract!

Now we're going to explore different ways of drawing our Mini-Me with these 7 Visual Elements of Style. First up is the Level of Realism!

ASSIGNMENT 9.2
Draw your Mini-Me in different levels of realism

1. Divide up and number your page into 9 sections, like this:

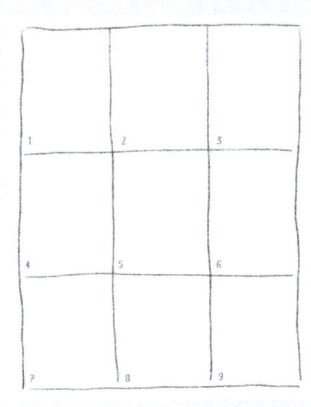

2. In the middle #5 section, redraw one of your Mini-Me drawings from Assignment 9.1 that you like the best.

3. That #5 Mini-Me now represents the middle on a scale of realism. In boxes 1-4, draw your Mini-Me more abstractly, and in boxes 6-9, draw your Mini-Me more realistically. In the end, you should have a range of your Mini-Me from the most abstract (#1) to the most realistic (#9).

Look back at *The 7 Visual Elements of Style* section for help.

Why We Did It

Deciding what level of realism you enjoy drawing most is a big step in developing your artistic style. Many people believe artists should always aim for realistic art, but that's only one way of drawing along a huge continuum. By exploring drawing both more and less realistically, you'll begin to find the level of realism that feels best to you!

Chapter 9: Refining Our Visual Style

ASSIGNMENT 9.3
Draw your Mini-Me with different linework

1. Divide up your page into 6 different sections, like this:

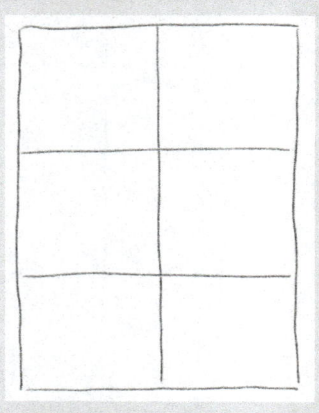

2. Draw your Mini-Me in each of the boxes, experimenting with different ways of using linework. Besides that, how you draw the Mini-Me is up to you. You'll most likely need to switch up your tools to experiment with different lines.

Look back at *The 7 Visual Elements of Style* section for help.

Why We Did It

By experiencing and exploring different ways of drawing lines, you will begin to find the linework that feels best to you!

ASSIGNMENT 9.4
Draw your Mini-Me with different colors

1. Divide up your page into 6 different sections, like this:

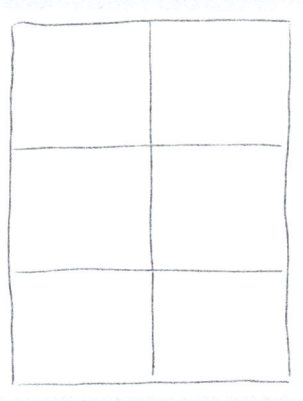

2. Draw your Mini-Me in each of the boxes, changing the colors you use with each one. Besides color, how you draw the Mini-Me is up to you.

Look back at *The 7 Visual Elements of Style* section for help. The color map there shows a range of colors within one hue, but you are welcome to use whichever and however many hues you want! You could explore monochromatic color too. We'll be experimenting with more specific color palettes in the Mood assignment.

Why We Did It

By experiencing and exploring different ways of using color in your art, you'll begin to find the colors that feel best to you!

Chapter 9: Refining Our Visual Style

ASSIGNMENT 9.5
Draw your Mini-Me with different form definitions

1. Divide up your page into 4 different sections, like this:

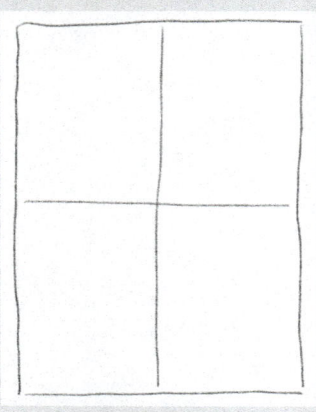

2. Draw your Mini-Me in each of the boxes, experimenting with different ways of defining form in each one. Besides that, how you draw the Mini-Me is up to you.

Look back at *The 7 Visual Elements of Style* section for help.

Why We Did It

By experiencing and exploring different ways of defining form in your art, you'll begin to find which form definition feels best to you!

ASSIGNMENT 9.6
Draw your Mini-Me with different uses of space

1. Divide up your page into 2 different sections, like this:

2. In the top section, draw your Mini-Me using a 2-D pictorial plane (one plane with minimal depth).

3. In the bottom section, draw your Mini-Me using a 3-D pictorial plane (multiple planes with more depth). You can add a foreground, middle ground, and background.

Look back at *The 7 Visual Elements of Style* section for help.

Why We Did It

By experiencing and exploring different ways of working with space in your art, you'll begin to find which way feels best to you!

Chapter 9: Refining Our Visual Style

ASSIGNMENT 9.7
Draw your Mini-Me with different textures

1. Divide up your page into 6 different sections, like this:

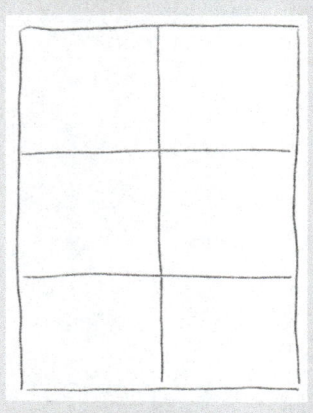

2. Draw your Mini-Me in each of the boxes, experimenting with different ways of drawing texture in each one. Besides that, how you draw the Mini-Me is up to you. You can explore different textures within mediums and also branch out into textures other tools produce.

Look back at *The 7 Visual Elements of Style* section for help.

Why We Did It

By experiencing and exploring different ways of working with texture in your art, you'll begin to find which textures feel best to you!

ASSIGNMENT 9.8
Draw your Mini-Me with different moods (color)

1. Divide up your page into 6 different sections, like the last assignment.

2. Draw your Mini-Me in each of the boxes, experimenting with different ways of conveying mood using color in each one. Besides that, how you draw the Mini-Me is up to you.

Look back at *The 7 Visual Elements of Style* section on color for examples of different color schemes to explore. What moods can you convey with color? How do certain colors make you feel?

While you're exploring how to communicate moods, also consider *which* moods you want to communicate. Which ones resonate most with you? We all go through different moods all the time! Here are some different examples of moods to explore:

- Cheerful and happy
- Melancholic and down
- Upset and grumpy
- Energetic and excited
- Calm and peaceful

Why We Did It

By experiencing and exploring different ways of communicating mood with color in your art, you'll begin to find which colors and moods feel best to you!

Chapter 9: Refining Our Visual Style

ASSIGNMENT 9.9
Draw your Mini-Me with different moods (story)

1. Divide up your page into 6 different sections, like the last assignment

2. Draw your Mini-Me in each of the boxes, experimenting with different ways of conveying mood using story in each one. Besides that, how you draw the Mini-Me is up to you.

Here are some examples of different story techniques to explore:

Just like with Assignment 9.8, keep thinking about WHICH moods you want to communicate. You can choose to work with the same moods from 9.8 or try out new moods.

Why We Did It

By experiencing and exploring different ways of communicating mood with narrative in your art, you'll begin to find which narrative techniques and moods feel best to you!

Style is Always Evolving

Even after you've found your Mini-Me, it will shift and evolve over time as you change. Sometimes in obvious literal ways, like if you shave off 13 inches of hair like I did one time. And sometimes in more subtle ways you may not even notice as you draw your character again and again, and as you grow and evolve as an artist.

And this goes for your *whole* style, not just your Mini-Me.

Just as you develop and become more like "you" as you grow up, your artistic style is doing the same thing. With every experience you have, you change and grow, and with every piece of art you make, your style changes and grows.

You don't have to stick with one static, unchanging artistic style for the rest of your life. Your style can and should change and evolve as you change and evolve. I don't know about you, but I'm a very different person now than I was 10, 5 or even 1 year ago. And my art is too.

You're still you, even when you change. And your style is still your style, even when it changes. Your style is just how you create your art. Everything you ever make will always be in your style, as long as you let it flow naturally.

Enjoy making your art, get in the zone, and follow your curiosity.

Chapter 9: Refining Our Visual Style

ASSIGNMENT 9.10
Draw your Mini-Me eating your favorite food

Alright! Nice work exploring all those visual elements of style! That was a lot of work and you're kickin' booty! Now let's draw your Mini-Me doing something fun, huh?

1. Turn to the next page in your sketchbook, and using whatever tools and elements of style you want, draw your Mini-Me eating your favorite food. You can start by drawing the food a few times by itself first. Then try drawing your character eating it!

2. Don't stop with just one drawing! Keep drawing your character eating that food in different ways, filling up the page.

Are you sitting down to eat? Standing up? Are you eating with your hands? A spoon? Chopsticks? Is it big? Small? Fill up the whole page however you like!

Why We Did It
We're stretchin' our legs with our Mini-Me and having some fun!

ASSIGNMENT 9.11
Draw a Mini-Me alphabet

1. Turn the page, and using your pencil, lightly draw the alphabet as large as you can fit onto the page. Think about how many letters there are, and how you can space them out in rows and columns to use the space of the page best. Draw as softly as you can, and try not to erase!

2. Now, with your fineliner or brush pen, draw your self-portrait character on top of the pencil in the shape of each letter.

For example, on top of the pencil letter A, you could draw your character bending over, forming the letter with their body, the arms making one branch of the A, legs making the other branch, hips making the tip, and their arm reaching across to make the bar in the middle of the A.

Step 3: Keep going, drawing your body to form the letters!

Why We Did It

This assignment helps us push the boundaries with our Mini-Me, encouraging us to think creatively and step out of our comfort zone.

I'M GRUMPY!
WOOLY
THAT'S REALLY NO GOOD.
UGH. I
UGH, I KNOW.
HA HA
WHY
HELP!
INKTOBER
TAY + VAL:
CHAOS
INHALE... EXHALE...
CLARIFY CALIBRATE OR CREATE
BROKEN
CHAOS.
FOLLOW THE DOG
C-O-N-N-E-C-T THE DOTS.
TRUST IN CHAOS.
HOW TO SAY SOMETHING

CHAPTER 10

Doing the Work

Developing a Creative Habit

There's only one thing you need to do to make something a habit: start doing it. And you've already started drawing, so you're well on your way to making it a habit! Now we just need to be able to stick with it and keep the habit going.

Drawing daily (or at least every other day) is the best way to build a drawing habit. But all this is easier said than done, so let's take a look at a couple of obstacles you might come across while you try to make drawing a habit.

"I don't have time to draw."

We're all busy. Our to-do lists are all overflowing, and we all say we "don't have time" for all the things we want to do. But drawing can fit into any schedule, no matter how busy you are. You don't have to draw for hours every day. Just 10 or 15 minutes each day will help you make drawing a habit and your skills will improve immensely. Even 5 minutes is better than none!

Just like with any habit, the beginning is the hardest. But once you make the time, and commit, drawing will become a habit, and you won't have to make yourself do it anymore. You'll want to do it, and just will.

You have to choose to make time for drawing.

Keep in mind that the amount of time you have to dedicate to drawing might ebb and flow over time. When I had my first child, I had to completely revamp my relationship with drawing. Then, once she was a toddler, I had to finagle my schedule all over again. I expect that I'll have to do that again and again throughout life—and that's ok!

Life is meant to fuel our art, not deter it. Having a child has given me more inspiration and motivation, even with the subtraction of free time. (For one thing, I'm much better at prioritizing and using my time wisely now.)

"I don't feel inspired."

This is a big one. A lot of people have trouble beginning to draw if they don't feel inspired. But if we only draw when we feel inspired, we won't draw very much at all!

To make drawing a habit, and to really improve, we have to draw regularly, even when we don't come to the page with tons of ideas and inspiration off the bat. This is really the difference between someone who takes drawing seriously and someone who just draws as an every-now-and-then occurrence.

So if you're having a hard time drawing with no inspiration, why not find your own inspiration?

Inspiration often comes from something outside ourselves. So try getting out of the house regularly and experiencing life! Try a new restaurant, walk down a different street, or talk to a new person. All these things can lead to new ideas and inspiration.

Or for an extra artistic boost, attend an art event! Go to an art show, an art museum, or even just browse your local art store. Even watching a thought-provoking or visually beautiful movie can spark the inner muse.

The point is, you need to pour stuff into yourself, absorbing the world around you and experiencing new things, if you expect to have consistent inspiration and ideas.

So get out there and live your life! It will make your art all the richer.

"I don't feel like drawing."

Don't feel guilty if there are days when you just don't feel like drawing. It does not mean you're not a real artist. Artists feel this way all the time—I feel this way all the time. Some days, you just don't feel like it.

But it's important to do it anyway. You need to draw, even when you don't feel like it. Consistent practice is the only way to improve and grow.

One way you can start drawing even when you don't feel like it is to remind yourself why you draw. Why are we doing this in the first place? Why is it so important?

Remember that drawing will make you feel calmer. It will make you feel more present. It will make you more creative. It will strengthen your skills. It will give you new ideas. It will wake you up and energize you. And it will help you find and know yourself!

Do you feel more like drawing now?

Chapter 10: Doing the Work

ASSIGNMENT 10.1
Add a block of drawing time to your calendar

1. Break out your calendar or however you keep track of your tasks and to-dos.

2. Pick a day this week you think you have a tiny bit of extra time.

3. Mark that block of time for drawing! Label it however you like: Drawing Time, Art Date, Sketchbook Party... whatever! Just block it off in your calendar. If you're using a digital calendar, you could set a reminder notification as well.

4. When that block of time actually comes up—stick to your guns! Draw during that period, even if just for a few minutes. You could do an assignment from this course, or draw whatever you want. Follow through!

Why We Did It

This assignment helps us make time for drawing, commit, and choose to prioritize drawing in our lives. Try to keep it going!

ASSIGNMENT 10.2
Draw a 6-panel comic about your day

1. Draw 6 panels and create a comic with your Mini-Me about the day you've had so far today.

That's it! That's the only instruction I have for you! This is an open-ended assignment for you to explore however you wish!

Why We Did It

We're practicing drawing with your Mini-Me and also with less instruction from me because we're getting towards the end of this book and you won't need me anymore!

Chapter 10: Doing the Work

Your Drawing Space

Having a space to draw can make a big difference in how often you draw. If you have to lug out all your pens and markers every time you want to draw, and then put everything up each time you're done, it makes drawing more of a chore and more difficult to start.

If you can, set up a space that is your drawing space only. I have a separate desk apart from my computer/work desk, that I only use for drawing. I leave my sketchbooks out and open, drawings strewn around, and my markers and pens scattered across the desk.

I've realized that having this desk makes it easier and quicker for me to start drawing, and reminds me to draw each day just by seeing all the sketchbooks and pens laying there!

I currently use our guest room as my studio with a dedicated drawing desk. But I didn't always have my own room like this, and have had many different dedicated drawing spaces that worked just as well! It's nice to have a room, but it's certainly not necessary.

You may not have the option of having a full room or even a desk for just drawing, and that's ok. But maybe there's a small space you could claim for your creativity? Even if it's just the corner of a room or the kitchen table after everyone's done with dinner?

Drawing Space Intruders

If you can't have a dedicated space, you may need to be a little more involved with dealing with distractions and intruders—er, I mean friends and family—while you draw.

One thing I like to do when I sit down to draw is put my phone on Do Not Disturb. You could also put on headphones so your family knows you're busy and to leave you alone for a bit. You may have to remind your housemates that you're going to have some me-time for a bit.

Having as little distraction as you can allows you to focus and get in the flow state much easier.

Chapter 10: Doing the Work

ASSIGNMENT 10.3
Set up your drawing space

1. Find a spot where you could set up your drawing space. It could be temporary, though hopefully, it could become your permanent art space. Whether it's a full desk, the corner of a room, or even just your side of the bed, try setting up a dedicated space today for you to draw.

2. Claim it for yourself! Put your sketchbook there, spread out all your pens and markers, and make a big ol' mess.

3. Try drawing there for a bit. If it works, keep going! If not, try somewhere new, until you find the spot that works for you.

Why We Did It

Having a dedicated space we can draw in helps us commit to our art practice, and makes it easier to sit down to draw regularly. Your tools and sketchbook will already be there, ready to go, and will remind you to draw when you see them as well.

Establishing a Routine

Finding What Works for You

Try to figure out what times you feel most creative and energetic, and draw during those times. Are you a morning person? Try waking up 30 mins early and use that time to draw in your sketchbook. More of a night owl? Try shutting down your phone and drawing in bed before you go to sleep instead of checking your email one more time. Or maybe drawing on your lunch break would give you a calming moment and creative boost during your work day at the office.

Try out different times and see when it's easier for you to start drawing.

I have the most energy in the mornings, so I tend to draw the best right after I drop my daughter off at school. I've found that during that time I'm most likely to be able to sit down and draw and have the mood, energy, and time to get into the zone.

Chapter 10: Doing the Work

ASSIGNMENT 10.4
Try to establish a drawing routine

1. Think about what time of the day you have the most creative energy. Try drawing at different times, and reflect on how easy/hard it was to figure out when you feel best.

2. Based on your most energized/creative time of day, set up and commit to following a drawing routine for a week. You don't have to stop this book, just try this on your own.

Just remember: We're aiming to draw every day. If you miss a day, it's ok. Life happens. Forgive yourself, let it go, and draw something today.

Why We Did It

Everyone feels most energized and creative at different times. If we can draw during those times, it will be easier for us to get started and we'll be more likely to stick with our creative habit. Just because all your favorite artists are night owls doesn't mean you have to be. Do what works for you!

Perfection Does Not Exist

Don't Let It Stop You From Starting

I hope by now you realize that doing the work is the most important thing. But often, we get down on ourselves. We feel like we aren't good enough, aren't improving, and aren't reaching that level of drawing we desperately want. And this mindset can be debilitating. It can stop us from starting. Stop us from doing the work. Stop us from drawing.

Please, don't let yourself fall into this trap. Don't let your thoughts or desire for perfection stop you from drawing. Forget about everything your inner critic tells you. Forget about all the bad drawings you think you've made. Forget about the mistakes you made. Forget about that artist you love who's so good and makes you feel you'll never be that good.

Forget about everything. Except drawing.

All you have to do is draw. Just do the work and the rest will come.

Chapter 10: Doing the Work

Assignment 10.5

Draw about your style journey

Ok, y'all—this is your last assignment! Can you believe it?! Let's do it!

1. Open your sketchbook to the next page. Using either your fineliner or brush pen, draw something about your journey to develop your style through this book.

You can choose to draw a panel comic, a one-page illustration, a doodle, or a drawing with lots of notes. You can choose to draw your biggest takeaway, the biggest thing you learned, what you gained from this experience, or how you feel about your style now. You could draw how you're style has changed or what you're excited to explore next.

Anything is up for grabs!

Woohoo! You Did It!

Congratulations! You've now completed the entire Sketchbook to Style book and filled up most, if not all, of your sketchbook! Celebrate and reward yourself!

I hope that over course of this book you developed a deeper love of drawing and feel more confident in your drawing style and communicating with your unique voice.

Developing your style is a lifelong process, so don't feel like you ever have to stay stuck where you are. You style will grow and change with you as you grow and change as a person.

Your art is special and the world needs more people who make art. Keep experimenting, keep exploring, and above all, keep drawing.

Thank you!

Thank you so much for purchasing and using this book, and I am so grateful for you choosing to take this journey with me.

I would love to connect more with you and see some of your assignments from this class or other artworks you've made! If you're interested, you can join my email newsletter at the URL below, which includes a chat group of other artists, drawing prompts, live online drawing events, and behind-the-scenes process work of my current books: *https://might-could.com/emails*

Well, that wraps up the book, and I really hope you enjoyed Sketchbook to Style!

Thank you again and keep on drawin'!

HEY! I DID THAT FIRST!
1984
ANIMAL FARM
THANK YOU!
THANK YOU
6
WHEW!
WHEW!
DAY9 Seattle
DAY8 Spokane
I'M SO TIRED...
ARE WE THERE YET?
THIS CITY IS NICE BUT I'M JUST SO TIRED...
WHAT AM I EATING? IS THAT SQUIRREL TALKING TO ME?
I AM JUST SO TIRED
DAY7 Beartooth Highway
DAY6 Fargo
DAY5 Minneapolis
MMM... THIS IS REALLY GOOD.
DAY 4 Madison
DAY3 Chicago
DAY3 Indiana
DAY2 Detroit MICHIGAN
The Motor City
DAY1 Ohio
HOW DO I DRAW
SHAVED HEAD AND
LOOK LIKE A BA

Resources

Oh, hey! You're still here! Cool, cool. Well, here are some bonus goodies and resources if you'd like to continue your artistic style journey!

On the following pages you'll find tear-out sheets and designs from various assignments. You can also find extra help for the assignments, sneak peeks at my own assignment drawings, a video flip-through of 15 years of my sketchbooks, plus lots more on my website:

www.might-could.com/sketchbook-to-style-resources

And you can join my email list here:

www.might-could.com/emails

Resources

Resources

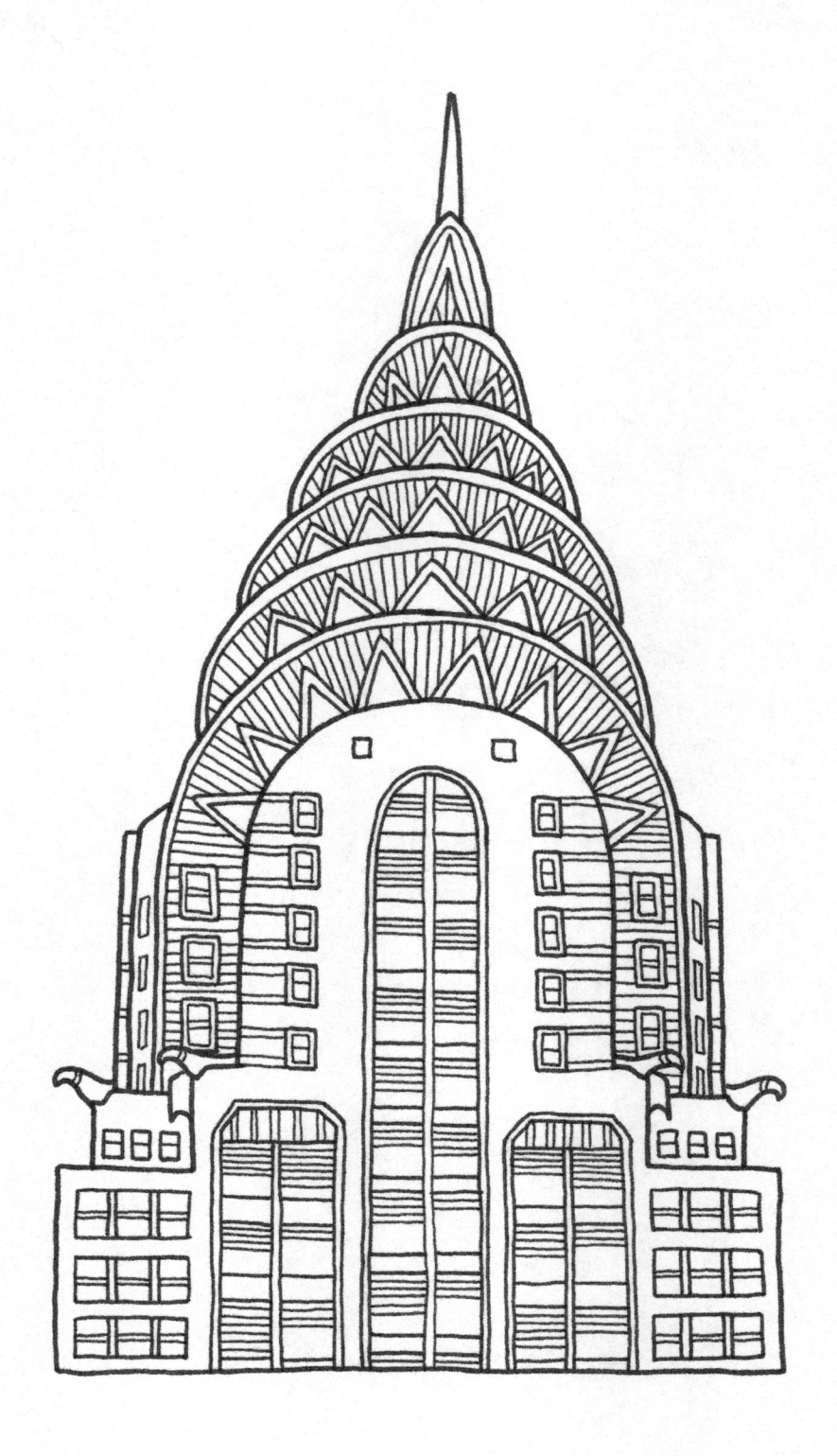

Resources

Resources

Resources

MAY
'18
NORTHEAST
ROAD TRIP
DAY 3
PHILADELPHIA!
PRINCETON!
NEW HAVEN!
DAY 10-16 VERMONT → GEORGIA → NORTH CAROLINA → GEORGIA
FAMILY IN VERMONT
GRANDMA
JOSIE
FAMILY BIRTHDAY
PAPA RALPH
GASTRONOMIC CONNOISSEUR!
PULLED PORK BBQ
ICECREAM
WEIRD OFF-BRAND SODAS
SOUTH CAROLINA CRABBING
LAWN MOWER
A VERY OLD, TINY BOAT
SAUSAGE EXTRAVAGANZA!
DAY 9 MONTRÉAL
JEAN-TALON MARKET
MONTREAL MUSEUM OF FINE ARTS
ICEHOUSE
DAY 8 MONTRÉAL
KOUIGN AMANN CAFÉ!
NOTRE-DAME
TITANIC
LIVERPOOL HOUSE
BIKING ALONG THE LACHINE CANAL
DAY 7 MONTRÉAL
MONTREAL
TEAM BISCUIT
FAMILY VACATION!
DAY 6 NEW HAMPSHIRE
CONWAY
DAY 5 PORTLAND, MAINE
LOBSTER SHACK!
CAPE ELIZABETH
TWO LIGHTS STATE PARK
PORTLAND HEADLIGHT
MAINE OYSTERS
CEVICHE
MAINE MUSSELS
DAY 4
RHODE ISLAND!

Made in the USA
Coppell, TX
23 May 2023